Leicest re

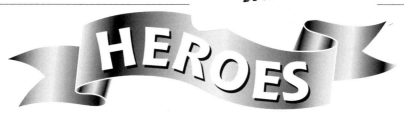

HEROES

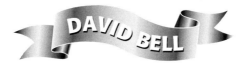

DAVID BELL

COUNTRYSIDE BOOKS
NEWBURY BERKSHIRE

First published 2005

COUNTRYSIDE BOOKS
3 Catherine Road
Newbury, Berkshire

To view our complete range of books,
please visit us at
www.countrysidebooks.co.uk

ISBN 1 85306 923 X
EAN 978185306 923 9

Designed by Peter Davies, Nautilus Design
Produced through MRM Associates Ltd., Reading
Typeset by Jean Cussons Typesetting, Diss, Norfolk
Printed by J. W. Arrowsmith, Bristol

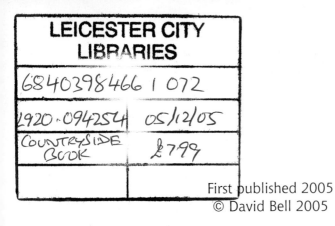

CONTENTS

CONTENTS

Introduction

I hope you enjoy reading this book about Leicestershire heroes. Some of them are household names, others are less well known than they should be. The collection is deliberately eclectic. All 24 people included are heroes to some Leicestershire residents, although it is almost certain that everyone who reads the book will at some time wonder why this hero is present but not that one. No one will disagree with the inclusion of Johnnie Johnson, the Spitfire ace who shot down 38 enemy planes during the war, or with Eliane Plewman, sent as an agent to wartime France and executed at Dachau. Another wartime hero is Philip Bent, promoted to Lieutenant Colonel by the age of 25, who won a posthumous VC at Passchendaele in World War I. Then there is Clare Hollingworth, the pioneering woman war correspondent.

Historical heroes are represented by traveller and adventurer Lady Florence Dixie, Thomas Cook, the travel organiser and temperance preacher, Robert Bakewell, who changed the face of English farming, suffragette Alice Hawkins, evolutionist Alfred Russel Wallace, George Fox, founder of the Quaker movement, and Mary Linwood, a celebrated artist in embroidery. A royal figure is Lady Jane Grey. Two Leicester characters, Daniel Lambert and Joseph Merrick, are deemed heroes because of the way in which they dealt with the physical deformities that a cruel fate had thrown at them.

Among my modern heroes are Alec Jeffreys, the inventor of DNA fingerprinting, Adrian Cross, the Antarctic sailor and campaigner, Sue Townsend, comic novelist sans pareil, and Linda Straw, a textile artist and a modern version of Mary Linwood. There are also two brothers from the world of film and television, David and Richard Attenborough, as well as Bob Miller, a fireman who lost his life in the service of others, and – controversially, perhaps – Malcolm Pinnegar, leader of Leicestershire's famous Dirty Thirty.

With sporting heroes, the selection is always contentious, but I have included Martin Johnson, captain of Leicester Tigers and England, who led his country to that wonderful Rugby World Cup victory against Australia in 2003. There is also Gary Lineker, son of a Leicester market trader, who scored forty-eight goals for England and never once in any club or international match earned a warning – red or yellow – from any referee. Jenny Pitman, who started life as a farmer's daughter in Hoby and became one of this country's most successful trainers of racehorses, completes my trio of sporting heroes.

Even if you disagree with one or two of my selection, I hope you will find plenty to enjoy.

David Bell

1

Johnnie Johnson

– Spitfire ace

I grew up in the Leicestershire town of Melton Mowbray, and back in the 1940s, when no one owned a car, we would often walk the mile or so into the town. From our home we would go down the long hill of Welby Lane, then onto Nottingham Road. I remember when I was a young lad of six or seven, my dad would point to the very last house on Welby Lane, just before the Welby Hotel, and say, 'That's Johnnie Johnson's house'. He told me that Johnnie was Britain's leading Spitfire pilot, and a real hero. 'He's shot down more enemy planes than any other pilot,' Dad would say with evident pride.

Johnnie Johnson is not just a Melton hero, as he was actually born in Barrow-on-Soar, so two Leicestershire locations claim him! He was not really Johnnie, either. Christened James Edgar, he was called Jim as a boy, but it was under his RAF nickname that he became world famous.

Johnnie's father was a police inspector and sent his son to Loughborough Grammar School and then to University College, Nottingham, where he took a degree in civil engineering. After university he went to work for Melton Urban District Council as an assistant in the Borough Surveyor's department. He was a keen Rugby Union player, and was very interested in learning to fly aeroplanes. In his early twenties, he was spending a fair proportion of his salary on flying lessons.

By now it was 1938, and the 22-year-old Johnnie could see that war with Germany was inevitable. Many of his rugby mates were joining the Territorials, but Johnnie decided to apply to join

Johnnie Johnson

the Auxiliary Air Force. His interview did not go too well, however. Johnnie stressed that he was taking private flying lessons but the officer who was interviewing him didn't seem impressed. Then, when he noticed that Johnnie was from Melton Mowbray, the officer, a keen foxhunting type, perked up and asked which hunt he was with. Johnnie tactfully said that all his spare cash was spent on flying, not hunting, after which the interview was speedily brought to an end. It is frightening to note that if the interviewer had had his somewhat bigoted way,

Johnnie Johnson would never have flown and this country would never have had the services of the legendary fighter pilot.

He next decided to apply to join the RAF Volunteer Reserve, which he described as 'far less of a *corps d'elite* than the socially inclined Auxiliary Air Force'. The RAFVR, formed in 1936, took in entrants at non-officer rank and trained them to fly, many of them getting commissions after gaining their wings. However, the Volunteer Reserve was getting far more applicants than they had vacancies, and he was told that there was no place for him at the moment but if the Reserve was expanded, they would get in touch.

Giving up the idea of joining the flying services, Johnnie decided to sign up to a Territorial outfit. Although he had no interest in hunting, he was an able horse-rider and he became a member of the mounted Leicestershire Yeomanry. Remembering his earlier disappointing interview with the Auxiliary Air Force, Johnnie wryly observed that he was glad that his troop commander didn't think it was necessary to be able to fly in order to ride a horse!

However, he then received a letter from the Air Ministry, saying that the Volunteer Reserve was being expanded, and he could now re-apply. He was accepted as a sergeant-pilot under training, and attended ground lectures and flying lessons in Tiger Moths on two evenings a week and at weekends. In August, after mobilisation, he was sent to Cambridge where he and his RAFVR colleagues found themselves lodged in very prestigious quarters, namely the Cambridge colleges of Jesus, Magdalene, Trinity and St John's.

His training continued at Sealand, near Chester, then at nearby Hawarden where he first flew Spitfires. There his instructors were seasoned pilots who had experienced fighting German Messerschmitts at Dunkirk and in the preliminary stages of the Battle of Britain. The instruction was all in flying, however, and

Johnnie Johnson and his fellow-trainees felt frustrated that they were not learning about fighting techniques.

In September 1940, with 205 flying hours in his log book, 23 of them in Spitfires, Johnnie was sent as a replacement pilot to 19 Squadron in Cambridgeshire, and then to 616 Squadron in Norfolk, where he met the young Squadron Leader, Billy Burton, a man Johnnie quickly came to both like and admire.

Johnnie rapidly became one of the most outstanding fighter pilots. Not only did he have excellent skills in handling his plane, he also had tremendous ability at deflection shooting. He had always shot rabbits as a youngster in Leicestershire, which may have helped. His first 'kill' was in June 1941 when, as Douglas Bader's wingman, he shot down a Messerschmitt 109. He shot down two more the following month, and a further two in September. These were the first of many.

Johnnie Johnson missed the Battle of Britain, due to an old rugby injury to his shoulder. A break in his collar bone had been badly set, and was now causing him pain and led to him packing cotton wool under the straps of his parachute harness. In addition, he was losing some feeling in his right hand, and having to land his plane using only his left. When this came to light, his CO gave him the choice of either moving to a permanent training role or having an operation and then returning to active flying duties.

His decision was predictable, and after the operation he set about making up for missing the dogfights of the Battle of Britain. He flew more than 1,000 wartime combat missions, and his total of 38 'kills' of enemy planes – 37 of which involved the shooting down of single-seater enemy fighter planes, fast and manoeuvrable, not the easier, slower bombers – made him the leading Spitfire pilot of the whole war. His tally of 38 is even more remarkable given that he missed the Battle of Britain where he would have undoubtedly added to the number. His own plane was only hit once, and he never had a plane shot down. He would be the first to claim an element of luck in this, but in truth his tremendous skill as a fighter pilot was the genuine reason for his so-called luck.

His ability didn't go unnoticed. In September 1941 he was promoted to Flight Lieutenant, and he became a Squadron Leader in 1942. In March 1943 he was given the rank of Wing Commander, and led the Canadian wing of the 2nd Tactical Air Force. He was awarded the DSO and two bars, the DFC and bar, the French Croix de Guerre and the Legion d'Honeur. After the war, he remained in the RAF and fought in the Korean War, where he was awarded the American DFC. He was awarded the CBE in 1960 and a CB in 1965. By the end of his career, Johnnie Johnson was an Air Vice Marshal, commander of RAF Middle East.

Johnnie Johnson retired from the RAF in 1966, and lived in neighbouring Derbyshire until his death in January 2001 at the age of 85. Tributes to J.E. Johnson included a flying display at RAF Cottesmore, where Johnnie had been Station Commander from 1957 to 1960. The display consisted of three Harriers flying in a 'Missing Man' formation, with a Spitfire owned by Rolls Royce. The Missing Man is a traditional flyers' tribute to a missing comrade, but the combination of Harriers and a Spitfire had never been flown before, and was a fittingly unique memorial to a unique man, a real Leicestershire hero.

2

Alice Hawkins

– trade unionist and militant suffragette

Alice Hawkins was born on 4th March 1863, one of the nine children of Henry Shaw, a travelling journeyman-shoemaker, but at some time during her early childhood her family settled in Leicester. Alice left school at the age of thirteen, to work in the boot and shoe trade, initially as a fitter who helped tighten the leather for the more skilled workers. She soon became aware that the women in the factory were paid far less than their male colleagues, and their working conditions were worse, too.

In her early twenties Alice found work at the Equity shoe factory on Friar's Causeway, a newly-founded workers' co-operative. The workers there were encouraged to join NUBSO, the National Union of Boot and Shoe Operatives, and to take part in political activity. In 1884 she married Alfred Hawkins, an active socialist, and together they had seven children. Family life did not tie Alice down, however. In 1892 she joined the Independent Labour Party and three years later she was forming and helping to run the ILP women's auxiliary organisation. The following year a Women's Co-operative Guild was started at the Equity shoe factory, and Alice was once again one of its leading members. She was elected as a NUBSO representative to Leicester Trades Council, and in 1905 she was involved in organising a protest march to London on the subject of unemployment.

By this time Alice was becoming somewhat disillusioned and disappointed with the trade union movement as a vehicle for improving the position of women. Alice had met members of the

Alice Hawkins (back left) and her five sisters

Pankhurst family in the 1890s, and again in 1905 when Christabel came to speak to the Leicester Trades Council, but it was February 1907 before she attended a meeting of their Women's Social and Political Union in London. Following the meeting in Hyde Park, the WSPU activists marched to the House of Commons to demand votes for women. Mounted police attacked the march, and Alice was one of the women arrested. She was charged with obstructing the police and sentenced to fourteen days in Holloway prison. This was her first taste of custody, but not her last.

The spell in prison did nothing to daunt the spirit of Alice and her colleagues. Supporters hired the London Excelsior Brass Band to play rousing music outside the gates, so that the women could hear it from their cells. They were released one by one at 9 am, presumably in the hope that they would creep away. The authorities couldn't have got it more wrong. As each prisoner was released, she was greeted by a cheering crowd of 200 well-wishers. They marched off into central London for a breakfast addressed by George Bernard Shaw, a leading supporter of their cause. At this breakfast, Alice read out a letter from her Leicester MP, Ramsay MacDonald. Although he expressed his regrets that Alice had been arrested, he also said that he thought the actions of the women would put back their cause. I can imagine that those women hearing his advice greeted it with loud disdain.

Alice returned to Leicester where, with the full support of her husband Alfred, she founded the Leicester Branch of the WSPU. Sylvia Pankhurst spent some time in Leicester that year, and she later wrote, 'At night I held meetings for the local WSPU, amongst whom only Mrs Hawkins as yet dared mount the platform.' While Sylvia Pankhurst was in Leicester she, not surprisingly, visited the Equity shoe factory. Sylvia was an artist and she drew a sketch in pastels of one of the Equity women workers. The picture is believed to be of Alice Hawkins, and in 2002 it was purchased at a Sotheby's auction for £9,400 by Leicester City Museums.

The Leicester branch of the WSPU began to campaign in the city and county, speaking in town squares, village greens and at factory gates. They called for women's suffrage, and frequently complained that the trade unions were not doing enough for their female members. They also tried to attend political meetings. In 1909, Alice was refused entry to a Liberal Party meeting held at the Palace Theatre, so her husband went inside in her stead while Alice protested outside. Alfred Hawkins interrupted the speaker – Winston Churchill – and demanded to know why the government refused votes for women. When he asked how Churchill dared stand on a democratic platform, Alfred was forcibly ejected from the meeting. When Alice and other supporters besieged the doors, asking to be allowed in, they were all arrested, and as Alice refused to pay a fine she was again sentenced to fourteen days, this time in Leicester prison. On this occasion she took part in a prison hunger strike along with a Helen Watts from the neighbouring county of Nottingham.

Alfred attempted to heckle Winston Churchill at another meeting, and he was attacked by violent stewards who threw him down a flight of steps. His leg was fractured and the Liberal Party was sued. He won his case and was awarded £100, a considerable sum in the first decade of the 20th century. Peter Barratt, the great-grandson of Alfred and Alice Hawkins, tells me that there is a family story that Alfred purchased an off-licence in Leicester with the compensation money.

Not all the listeners to Alice's speeches were sympathetic. On one occasion she was speaking in Leicester's Market Place when a heckler shouted that she should get off home to her family. She was able to smile and point to Alfred and her teenage children by her side. 'Here they are,' she said with understandable pride. 'They are my supporters.' The Leicester authorities tried to use this antipathy and violence from some elements of the crowd to dissuade Alice from addressing open-air meetings, but she refused to accept this. Her Leicester meetings attracted large numbers of people, both pro and anti, and had to be attended by a police presence. Alice was not just an activist in her home area. In 1908 she addressed a massed meeting of 250,000 supporters in Hyde Park, and in *The Times* of the next day she was described as a keynote speaker.

Unlike the Pankhurst family, Alice was definitely a working-class woman, living in a very ordinary area of Leicester. When she was needed for a meeting in London, the Pankhursts would send a car for her. Her neighbours must have been amazed when a huge chauffeur-driven vehicle managed to make its way down the back streets of Leicester to pick her up.

Alice Hawkins served three further prison sentences for breaking windows – including one at the Home Office for which she got 21 days – and for pouring red ink into pillar boxes in Leicester's Granby Street. She frequently refused to eat while in prison. Suffragettes often used prison hunger strikes as part of their protests, and were force fed so violently that they had their teeth knocked out.

Dissatisfied with the unsympathetic attitude of NUBSO, Alice and a colleague, Lizzie Wilson, formed a trade union for female workers in the boot and shoe factories – the Independent National Union of Women Boot and Shoe Workers. Founded in 1911, this union continued in existence until the 1930s. Alice lived in Leicester for the rest of her life, and died at the age of 83, a lifelong supporter of Labour and the trade union movement. On her death in March 1946, the *Leicester Mail* headline was: CITY SUFFRAGETTE DEAD: JAILED FIVE TIMES IN FIGHT FOR WOMEN'S VOTE. It is not surprising that she is one of Leicester's favourite daughters, a genuine Leicester hero.

Peter Barratt's mother, Alice's granddaughter, is now in her eighties and she often tells her son, 'My grandmother said to me when I was a teenager, "You must use your vote, we suffered for it," and I always have.' Peter regards that as a lesson we should all heed. He is very proud of his descent from this feisty lady. 'She was a determined and valiant woman,' he tells me, 'who stood up for what she believed in.' He is proud of his great-grandfather Alfred too, adding, 'Throughout her time as a suffragette, Alice benefited greatly from the strong support of her husband and of her employer.'

There is a blue plaque in honour of Alice Hawkins on the wall of the Equity shoe factory in Western Avenue, and the sketch of Alice by Sylvia Pankhurst will eventually be displayed at a Leicester museum.

'Suffragette' was originally a term of contempt coined by the *Daily Mail*, but it was picked up and used by the more militant women. 'Suffragist' was the term used by the less militant supporters – men or women – who campaigned for women's votes.

Another Leicester suffragette was machinist Ellen Sherriff. She was in favour of direct action to achieve the vote and she slipped out of her home in the middle of the night of 12th July 1914. With a colleague, Ellen set fire to Blaby's wooden railway station. Although it was known that suffragettes had caused the conflagration – they had left copies of their newspaper *The Suffragette* – the two culprits were never discovered. It was not until after Ellen's death that her nephew Harry Murby felt able to publicise his aunt's action. 'The Leicester suffragettes were split into two groups, the peaceful ones and the militant ones,' he said, 'and Ellen was a militant one.'

Carole Claridge from Hinckley recalls her great-aunt Gracie Ball who began working for the cause of women's suffrage, chaining herself to railings at the age of sixteen. Unlike the family of Alice Hawkins, Gracie's relatives were shocked by her actions, especially when she was sent to prison. Gracie was disowned by her family, and died in poverty in the workhouse in 1928.

The fight of women like Alice Hawkins, Ellen Sherriff and Gracie Ball led to women being given the vote in 1918. Discrimination still prevailed, however, and only women over 30 were given the franchise, compared with men who could vote at the age of 21. It was not until 1928 that they achieved parity with male voters.

3

Adrian Cross

– campaigning environmentalist with a worldwide reputation

Adrian Cross was born in 1952 in the Leicestershire town of Ashby-de-la-Zouch, which despite the old pre-war comic song *Ashby-de-la-Zouch-by-the-sea*, is about as far from the sea as it is possible to get. Nevertheless, Adrian is now one of our most well travelled sailors and also an environmentalist who is respected worldwide. He was the third in a family of seven, six of them boys. Born in Ashby, he actually grew up in the nearby village of Heather. At Ibstock Secondary School, he was held back by his dyslexia though he was keen on art and drama. 'On leaving school', he told me, 'I was faced with three choices: working in a factory, on a farm, or going down the pit like my dad.'

He actually avoided all three, because at the age of fifteen, he and two friends went to the careers office in Leicester, intending to join the forces. 'One intended to join the army, one the RAF, and I wanted the join the navy,' he recalls. Although the other two didn't succeed, Adrian did and he spent the next twelve years as a sailor. He trained at HMS *Ganges*, then transferred to Arbroath, where he gained his Junior Coxswain certificate at 16 years old. He began to develop an interest in sports of various kinds, taking up rugby, sailing, shooting, swimming and boxing. He was also interested in climbing and became a member of the mountain rescue team in the Cairngorms. At the age of sixteen and a half he went to HMS *Hermes*, an aircraft carrier, as a 'monkey boy,' part of the crane crash crew, dealing with removing crashed planes from the deck. Often this involved using a crane to pick up burning planes and dropping them over the side.

ADRIAN CROSS

Adrian Cross

The year 1971 found him on the Falkland Islands with a hovercraft unit. At that time he enjoyed shooting birds and animals. 'We shot everything in sight,' he admits, 'particularly geese.' Because the birds were regarded as a pest, Adrian and his fellow sailors could get a few pence every time they handed in a goose beak, but usually gave the birds to local families, who would invite the young sailors to lunch in return. 'I was a big supporter of hunting and shooting in those days,' Adrian says.

His attitude began to change when a friend in the Marines gave him a camera. Although it didn't have a telescopic lens, he found that the local birds and animals were so unafraid of human beings that he could get very close to them, taking some wonderful photographs. Adrian discovered he had a real talent for photography and he persuaded many of his friends to swap their guns for cameras. They photographed albatrosses, skuas, elephant seals and penguins. He even had a pet penguin for a while, which was actually one that adopted him and followed him everywhere. He also took photos of the Falklands bays and cliffs, many of which were unmapped. A decade later, during the Falklands war, he handed in these photos and thinks it possible that they were used in the planning of the assault on Port Stanley. He certainly didn't get his pictures back until after the war was over.

After a spell on loan to RAF Cottesmore, he became an engineer with a commando helicopter squadron in northern Norway. As part of the Mountain and Arctic Warfare Cell, Adrian's role was teaching people to survive in arctic conditions. One of his students was Prince Charles.

When he came out of the forces, he came back to north-west Leicestershire and fulfilled a dream of working in aircraft engineering for British Midland at East Midlands Airport. He had a second job driving trucks, and says that for a while he worked so hard that all his other interests and hobbies came to a stop.

Nine years later, another big change occurred when Adrian left aviation and entered the world of investments and insurance. After a spell at a firm in Ashby, and for the first time in his life sitting and passing exams, he became an accounts consultant at Standard Life. In his words, 'My job was advising the advisors.' He once more took up sport, particularly rugby and marathon running. He also entered the world of local politics. Having been a union shop steward at the airport, he now found himself first a district councillor in Coalville, then a Leicestershire county councillor. He was very interested in environmental issues, and was active in banning the use of certain toxic pesticides near schools and getting beef taken off the schools dinner menus when BSE first raised its ugly head. He was part of the early planning for the National Forest, and in dealing with the outbreak of algae bloom on Rutland Water.

He also became very involved in the discussions about foxhunting. Leicestershire County Council owned a lot of farmland, and was wondering whether to ban hunting on its land. With his interest in long distance running, Adrian even volunteered to become the quarry in drag hunts, if the local hunts would make the switch. 'But they basically told me to get lost,' he says. 'After their arrogant attitude, I became more passionate in my views and was even named as a public enemy in the *Horse and Hounds* magazine!' Adrian was opposed to both hare coursing and foxhunting, and helped uncover illegal artificial fox-earths and feeding pens in the Market Harborough area, the existence of which had been vehemently denied by the hunting fraternity.

Adrian and his colleagues on the county council did manage to ban foxhunting on council owned land, but the ban had to be rescinded on legal advice, following an appeal court ruling on a similar ban on staghunting on Exmoor. 'They were exciting times!' Adrian says with a rueful smile.

By now Adrian had rekindled his interest in sailing, and he became an instructor at Staunton Harold Reservoir. When he saw a notice in the Standard Life in-house magazine, inviting people to volunteer for secondment for two months working in the Antarctic, he applied. He had always been interested in Antarctica, ever since being told stories about the explorer Shackleton by his music teacher at school. In the Falklands, he had sat looking south and dreaming of getting there one day. Eventually he found himself being interviewed in Edinburgh by Robert Swan OBE, the explorer and environmentalist. 'Robert Swan was the first man to walk to both the north and south poles,' Adrian told me recently, 'and he was – and is – a great hero of mine.' Obviously, our heroes have heroes, too!

When he went for his interview, Adrian took with him a video of him teaching youngsters to sail, and after watching it, Robert asked him, 'Are you a leader or a team player?' Adrian thought quickly and said he could be either. 'I'd have been whatever he wanted,' he laughs. A year later, in 1999, Robert Swan sent for Adrian, and he found himself leading six complete strangers, none of them sailors, on the *Pelagic*, a 55-ft yacht, heading for Antarctica. 'We did have an experienced skipper,' he explains.

The party, a mixture of young people from Holland and the UK, flew out to Argentina, then sailed via the Beagle Channel to Cape Horn. From there it was a 600-mile voyage south to Antarctica, being accompanied for part of the way by whales, much to the delight of Adrian and his crew. After calling at King George Island, they made their way to a Russian scientific base at Bellingshausen. 'They made us very welcome,' he recalls. 'We had the complete run of the place, and used their radio equipment to send home the message that we had all arrived safely.' All the scientific bases had entered an agreement to remove from Antarctica all debris and rubbish caused by human beings. Part of Adrian's mission was to help the Russians by photographing, measuring, mapping and assessing the rusting metal containers, vehicles and so on that littered the area around the base. As much as 1,000 tons of waste metal and other rubbish was removed two years later and taken to Uruguay for recycling.

After leaving Bellingshausen, the second part of the expedition was spent photographing the wonderful wildlife, whales, seals and penguins, and in recording the effects of global warming on the Antarctic environment. All the time they were responsible for the upkeep of the *Pelagic*, and Adrian was delighted when they managed to replace a failed water pump, which kept the engine from overheating. Fortunately, he did have a spare on board! They visited the remains of an old whaling station on Deception Island, a volcanic site where steam and hot water come up through the ice, and also an historic British expeditionary base at Port Lochroy.

From time to time they saw luxury cruise ships bringing wealthy tourists to Antarctica. There was some debate on board as to whether this was a good development or not, but the consensus was that at least it might help to make more people aware of the devastating effects of global warming. After the journey back to the southern tip of South America, the crew parted. The six crew members had become a close unit. Adrian tells me that part of the delight he finds in his new life is the way that all nationalities, Dutch, Russians, Americans, British and many others, combine in a common cause.

Adrian has continued to work for the environment, talking to schoolchildren about Antarctica and instructing young sailors. In 2000 he was awarded a certificate, naming him a special envoy of the United Nations Educational, Scientific and Cultural Organisation, in recognition of his outstanding work with Mission Antarctica.

In 1999 Adrian decided to take a career break and his employers, Standard Life, granted him three and a half years' unpaid leave. He bought a boat of his own, an ocean-going yacht, which he named *Gentoo of Antarctica* (a gentoo is a penguin). With the aid of volunteer friends and colleagues he completely renovated the boat and set off on a round-the-world journey. On the first part he took with him a local artist, Fred Griffiths of Ibstock. A severe storm in the Bay of Biscay caused the yacht some damage, and when Adrian got to Spain he was able to check the *Gentoo*. The damage was even worse than he feared and had to abandon the voyage, for the time being, at least.

Hearing that Adrian was back in the UK, Robert Swan then gave him a job, back in Antarctica, setting up an education centre for students on an extreme leadership course. He then took a party of South African youngsters on a journey, sponsored by Coca-Cola, that circumnavigated the African continent, to raise awareness of the dangers of HIV, one of his main causes. He is rightly proud of the part that Robert Swan and his colleagues played in persuading the international drug companies to bring down the price of HIV drugs in Africa.

In 2004 the adventurer-explorer was back in Antarctica, in the footsteps of his childhood hero Shackleton, helping to build a yurt village (a yurt is a Mongolian style hut). When I spoke to Adrian at his Thringstone home in June 2004, he was just about to depart for South Africa to pick up a yacht and sail it to Australia. He was also actively planning another continental circumnavigation, namely a journey round North and South America, which would involve sailing through the legendary Northwest Passage.

For me, Adrian Cross is a man who has changed his life. Once a hunting-shooting-fishing enthusiast, he is now a campaigning environmentalist with a worldwide reputation. He has been in the Royal Navy, an aircraft engineer, an insurance accounts adviser, an active politician, an Antarctic explorer, a youth leader, a yachtsman. It is hardly surprising that I include this multi-faceted man in this book of Leicestershire heroes.

4

Lady Jane Grey

– Queen for nine days

Lady Jane Grey was born in 1537 at Bradgate Hall, Leicestershire. Her royal connections, which led to her rise to the highest position in the land and also to her untimely death, came about through her maternal grandmother, Mary Tudor. Mary was the younger sister of Henry VIII, and when she was in her early teens Henry had married her off to the 52-year-old Louis XII of France, as a useful alliance. Louis died only eleven

The ruins of Bradgate Hall, once the home of Lady Jane Grey
(courtesy of Lesley Hextall)

weeks after the marriage and Henry decided to have his sister brought back to England, in order to use her for a second diplomatic marriage. He sent his friend Charles Brandon – his tennis partner – to bring Mary back, plus as much of her marriage dowry as possible. When Brandon met Mary, bells rang, music played, and the couple took an instant fancy to one another. By the time they were back in England, they were madly in love and had taken part in a secret marriage. They were playing with fire. Marriages among royalty were for making alliances, not a matter of passion or romance. Henry flew into a towering rage and could easily have had both of them executed. However, after a few weeks of ranting and raving, he relented and, giving them the title of Duke and Duchess of Suffolk, allowed the marriage to stand. The daughter of this marriage, Frances, married Leicestershire's Henry Grey. At first the Greys lived at Groby Manor, then at their newly built home Bradgate Hall. The eldest of their three daughters was Lady Jane Grey.

Lady Jane Grey grew up in Leicestershire to be a bright attractive girl, speaking seven languages. Her royal connections, however, led her to be used as a pawn by powerful men in their pursuit of their ambitions. Henry VIII had died leaving his sickly son Edward on the throne, with his sisters Mary and Elizabeth the next in line. Mary, of course, had remained true to the Catholic faith of her mother, Catherine of Aragon, and many courtiers feared what would happen if she succeeded her brother to the throne. The young girl from Leicestershire was seen as a possible route to the throne. When Jane was nine, she was sent to stay with Katherine Parr, the widow of Henry VIII. Katherine Parr's new husband, Thomas Seymour, devised a plan to marry young Jane to King Edward, but when Katherine Parr died in childbirth, Jane returned to her parents' home. When Seymour was executed for treason, the Greys kept their heads down and were lucky to avoid being involved.

LADY JANE GREY

The next ambitious powerbroker to use Jane Grey was John Dudley, the Earl of Northumberland. He knew that if Edward died young and Mary became Queen, his power would be severely curtailed. It might be possible to oppose Mary's succession because Henry VIII had declared her illegitimate, maintaining that he was never legally married to her mother. However, this presented a problem: Henry had also declared Elizabeth illegitimate because of her mother's alleged adultery. Northumberland's eye fell on Lady Jane Grey, and he persuaded her willing parents to agree to her marrying his 19-year-old son. When Jane was told of the wedding – a week before the ceremony – she refused to listen, until she was thrashed into submission by her father. The wedding took place in London on Whit Sunday 1553, at a triple ceremony, with her 13-year-old sister and Northumberland's own daughter being married at the same time. Despite having been promised that she could return to Bradgate Hall after the ceremony, Northumberland now told Jane that she must remain in London ready to become Queen if the King should die. Jane thought that this was just a plot to keep her from going home. She was very unhappy and spent the next few weeks hiding from her new husband.

Edward, who had been persuaded to name Jane as his heir, died on 6th July, at the age of sixteen. When Jane was informed that she was now Queen she fainted in terror and shock. When she came round, she prayed that if it was her duty to succeed to the throne she should gain the courage to do so well. She was crowned on 10th July 1553, at the Tower of London. The first demand of Northumberland to the new Queen was that she declare his son to be King. She refused, saying that she could make him a duke, but only Parliament could make him King. This is an indication that had she kept her crown, Jane may not have proved the puppet her father-in-law was expecting. After all, she did have Tudor blood in her veins.

Unfortunately, the people did not support young Queen Jane; they knew that Mary – despite her religious views – was the rightful heir to the throne. An army of 30,000 soldiers marched towards London in Mary's support, and she was proclaimed Queen in the town of Norwich. Faced with this popular support, Northumberland left London for Cambridge where, in a spectacular volte-face, he declared himself a Catholic and a supporter of Queen Mary. All the nobles who had been present at Jane's coronation now declared themselves for Mary. This included Lord Grey, Jane's own father. Mary rode into London in triumph, with her sister Elizabeth at her side, and the reign of Queen Jane ended nine days after it had begun.

Northumberland's change of religion did not do him much good. Mary had him tried and executed; as an arch-plotter himself, Northumberland may or may not have appreciated the fact that his judges included many who had been his co-conspirators, now anxious to prove themselves true supporters of Queen Mary.

Jane and her husband were imprisoned in the Tower, and it is probable that Queen Mary would have pardoned them after a year or two, as long as they retired to the country. However, within a few months, Jane's father had involved himself in Sir Thomas Wyatt's rebellion against Mary's intended marriage to the King of Spain. Mary decided that she could be merciful no longer; Lady Jane Grey and her husband were sentenced to be executed on 12th February 1554. Lord Dudley went to the scaffold on Tower Hill, but as a person of royal blood, Jane Grey – Queen for nine days – was beheaded within the walls of the Tower. She was sixteen at the time of her death.

There is a legend that Lady Jane Grey killed the last wolf in Leicestershire. When she was fourteen or fifteen, she was out walking, it is said, with young Francis Beaumont of Grace Dieu Hall. The wolf attacked them and wounded Francis, and knocking

Lady Jane Grey's execution (courtesy of Joe Pie Picture Library)

him to the ground. Courageously, Jane attacked the wolf and killed it by forcing a tree branch into its open mouth. It is quite possible that young Francis and Lady Jane Grey had romantic feelings for each other, but this was a relationship that was doomed to be unsuccessful. Jane's own feelings had no part in the plans of her ambitious father. He saw her on the throne of England, not marrying some minor Leicestershire noble. His intrigues not only lost her the possibility of marrying her childhood sweetheart, but also cost Jane her life.

5

Alfred Russel Wallace

– naturalist and early natural selection theorist

Alfred Russel Wallace, a teacher at the Collegiate School in Leicester in the 1840s, was fascinated with the subject of natural history. In the 1850s, Wallace travelled to the Malay Archipelago and to South America, to study the flora and fauna, and to gather specimens. On a visit to the Amazon rain forest in 1858, he went down with malaria. In a state of delirium, all his thoughts and theories came together, and with a sudden flash of fever-inspired revelation, he realised that organisms that are best adapted to their surroundings have a better chance of surviving to reproduce. He had come up with the concept of the survival of the fittest.

Wallace wrote a paper about this and sent it to a fellow enthusiast, Charles Darwin. Wallace asked Darwin to read the paper, then send it on to the famous geologist Charles Lyell. Darwin, who had been thinking along the same lines for twenty years but had not yet published his ideas, contacted Charles Lyell, and he arranged for both Wallace's written essay and Darwin's unpublished writings to be presented to a scientific society. This spurred Darwin into action, and his work *The Origin of Species* was published just over a year later.

So did Charles Darwin steal the Leicester teacher's ideas? Not really. Both men were working on the same lines, and both came up with the theory of evolution. Moreover, Charles Darwin always acknowledged his debt to the researches of Alfred Russel Wallace. Indeed Darwin once said that Darwinism should really be called 'Wallacism'.

6

Martin Johnson

– international rugby legend and inspirational captain

Martin Johnson was born in the West Midlands but came to Leicestershire with his family when he was seven years of age. His relationship with his adopted county has lasted ever since. His father David, an engineering graduate, had worked at Lucas Industries, but in 1977 he took a job at Tungstone Batteries in Market Harborough. The family – David, Hilary and their three young sons – moved to a house in Burnmill Road on the northern outskirts of Market Harborough.

Martin, the middle son, found himself at Ridgeway Primary School, and turned his attention to playing soccer. He would join in the kickabout game on the netball pitch before school, at morning playtime, at lunchtime and after school. Martin says that the tarmac surface was covered in pea gravel, which would embed itself in your flesh and skin your knees whenever you fell over. The process of toughening up obviously began early. Within a couple of years, Martin was in the school soccer team as a centre back, and he ended up as the team captain. Teachers at neighbouring schools began to ask about the huge boy who had played for Ridgeway Primary for three years, and could he really be still only 11 years old? Fiercely competitive, Martin had very different ideas from his teacher who would select any boy who turned up to the practices, regardless of ability. Martin wanted to win and that meant the best players only. Martin was also playing regularly for Harborough Town Juniors.

In 1980 his dad, who had occasionally played rugby for Orrell, took him to Twickenham to see an international rugby union

Martin Johnson (courtesy of the *Leicester Mercury*)

match, England v Wales. Martin noticed that four of the England players, including Clive Woodward and Dusty Hare, actually played for Leicester. He began to watch rugby on television and to chat to boys at school whose families took them to watch Leicester Tigers. When he went on at aged eleven to Welland Park High School, he was able to play both rugby and soccer. However, the school soccer team wasn't as successful as the rugby team, so he began to veer towards the XV-man game. Martin was big for his age and soon found himself wearing the number 8 shirt, positioned in the back row, when Welland Park played against other local schools. The school was able to obtain free schoolboy tickets to Leicester Tigers matches, and Martin and his brother began to go to watch about ten matches per season.

Students in Leicestershire transfer from high school to upper school at fourteen, and Martin started at Robert Smyth School in 1984. There, inter-house rugby was played, though there was not much of a school team, but by now Martin was playing for Leicestershire under-14s. He now had a dilemma. Most of his rugby mates went on to play for Wigston RUFC, but Martin was still turning out on Saturday afternoons to play soccer for Harborough Town. He had to choose between the two sports. He decided to go with rugby and began to turn out regularly for Wigston. At fifteen, he was playing for the colts, the under-19 team, and, after swapping his position from back row to lock, he was selected for the Midlands area team and then for the England under-18s.

He became conscious of the public school old boys' network when a team-mate, Neil Back, 'the best player in the team', was dropped to make room for a public schoolboy with connections to the coaching set-up. In Martin's own words, 'It was my first taste of the garbage that surrounded English rugby for far too many years.'

Surprisingly, although Martin was playing at national level and lived just fourteen miles down the A6, he was never approached to sign for the Leicester Tigers. In the end he decided to simply turn up at the Tigers' Welford Road ground and ask to train with them. He was soon selected to play for their youth team. His Leicester Tigers career had begun, although he didn't know it. Rugby was an amateur game, just a hobby; you couldn't make a living at it, could you?

In 1989 Martin had left school and was doing odd jobs on a building site. He was wondering whether to try to become a PE teacher like his mum, when he received a very odd letter from New Zealand. John Albert, a Maori who had seen Martin playing in a three-way tournament in Australia, was inviting him to come out to New Zealand to play for his local rugby team, Tihoi. He would pay for Martin's airfare, find him a job, and give him a place in the team. Martin was nineteen and had no ties, so he decided to give it a go. Once there, he lodged with John and his family, and was found a job in a local bank. He played for Tihoi, but was also soon offered a place in the King Country provincial team, playing against top teams, which included Auckland, Canterbury and Wellington.

At one of the post-match barbecues, Martin met Kay Gredig, the daughter of one of the Tihoi club directors, and it was not long before she was his girlfriend. A pretty girlfriend and playing rugby in New Zealand! Could life get any better?

Well, it could. Martin was invited to an All Blacks under-21 trial, some compliment for a teenager from England. After a second trial, he was selected for the squad, and went on tour in Australia. His team managed to beat the Wallabies under-21 team in a very physical junior test match in Sydney. Martin could well have had a career as a member of the All Blacks but, after eighteen months in New Zealand, he made the big decision to come home to Leicestershire. It was a big wrench, but he did bring Kay with him. They were actually to marry ten years later.

Martin arrived back in Leicestershire in October 1990, and was offered a game for Tigers thirds, then played twice in the seconds. He was given a game in the first XV in a cup match at Bath, which the Tigers were not expected to win. In a mudbath of a game, Tigers did win and the press began to notice Martin Johnson. He was the new boy in the team, and the fact that he was a local boy who had played for the All Blacks in New Zealand gave them an extra angle.

Having gained a place in the full Tigers team, Martin was hit by a setback. A recurrent left shoulder injury, which had been misdiagnosed as a tendon problem, turned out to be a dislocation. His shoulder had been popping out regularly during matches and Martin had been simply been pushing it back in to carry on playing. Once correctly identified – by the opposition's physio at a match against the Barbarians – this problem involved him undergoing a couple of operations, and Martin lost a whole season's rugby. It was the 1992-3 season before he was back, but now he was commanding a regular spot in the team. He was also selected, as a last minute replacement for Wade Dooley, for an England v France match at Twickenham. In this match, Martin was concussed after a head clash with the French prop, but he played on and England won by a single point.

His subsequent career has led Martin Johnson to become an international rugby legend, a sporting giant both literally and metaphorically. The physical giant is 6 ft 6 ins in height, 17 stone in weight, and takes a size 14 shoe! As a player in over 300 games, and from 1997 as captain, he has helped to turn Leicester Tigers into the world's most successful club side, winning cups and Premier League championships year after year. In two consecutive years, 2001 and 2002, Leicester Tigers were winners of the Heineken Cup, beating Stade Francais and Munster respectively in the finals, making Tigers the champions of Europe.

As captain of England from 1999, Martin led England to some mighty victories, and the BBC recently described him as the dominant British player of modern times. Over eleven years, he won 84 international caps, and led England to Triple Crowns, Grand Slams and the World Cup. To summon up a few matches as memorable is difficult; there are so many. In one away match against New Zealand in June 2003, England was hanging on to a slender lead with ten minutes to go, when two of their players – Neil Back and Lawrence Dallaglio – were sin-binned. It was now thirteen men against fifteen, but captain Martin Johnson urged his five remaining forwards to out-push their eight opponents. England won the match 15-13, and Clive Woodward, the England coach, described Martin's leadership as inspirational. 'In that ten minute period you saw Martin Johnson at his absolute best,' he declared.

Perhaps the match remembered by most people is the World Cup Final against Australia in November 2003. At 17 points each, and with seconds to go, Martin inspired his players for one final push and set up a position for Johnnie Wilkinson to drop a winning goal. Wilkinson was rightly glorified and lauded for his kicking, but rugby fans knew that Martin Johnson had been the commanding powerhouse – dominating in lineouts and physically unbeatable in all his exchanges – who had made the victory possible. Both Johnnie Wilkinson and Martin Johnson were awarded CBEs for their part in winning the World Cup, Martin having been made an OBE in 1997. Martin quit international rugby after this, and England certainly misses his inspirational captaincy. He also retired from club rugby at the end of the 2004-5 season. His last game at Welford Road was against Wasps on 30th April 2005. Tigers and Wasps were lying first and second respectively in the Zurich Premiership, and Martin led his team to a 45-10 victory. Leicester Tigers, like England, will miss him both as a player and as a captain.

Martin was always a strong supporter of the move for Rugby Union to become a professional game. He thought it wrong that players in England, unlike those from the southern hemisphere, should be handicapped by needing to have a job and to play rugby in their spare time. While his own employers, the Midland Bank, were always very generous with time off, others were not so lucky. Dean Richards, a Leicester policeman, would do a nightshift, grab an hour's sleep, spend the day on rugby related activities, then go straight off for another night's work. Darren

Garforth would race straight to play for the Tigers after working as a scaffolder on a building site in Coventry, arriving only minutes before the kick-off. Martin was also keen that ability should be the only criterion for selection, with 'public school connections' playing no part. He does admit that there were one or two players who nominally supported professionalism, but who were unwilling to put in daily training once it was achieved. They didn't last long, he recalls. They were not fit enough to keep their place in the teams, and were replaced by players who did the full-time preparation.

One of the tributes paid to Martin was to have a full-length portrait painted by the renowned portrait painter Bryan Organ. The picture, which is a massive 5 ft 6 ins by 4 ft 4 ins, took four months to complete. It shows Martin in his Tigers kit, standing hands on hips at the Welford Road ground, looking both thoughtful and brooding. His expression is somewhere between a smile and a glower. The artist, who has painted portraits of several members of the royal family, told one critic that the hardest task when creating Martin's portrait was to convey the many different facets of his character and to distil an image of both a warrior and a gentleman. After being on show at Leicester Art Gallery and Museum for a period, the painting is now on permanent display at the Tigers' rugby ground. It is a magnificent portrait of a colossal Leicestershire sporting hero.

7

Clare Hollingworth

– pioneering war correspondent

Clare Hollingworth was born in 1911 in Knighton, then a village south of Leicester. During the First World War her family moved to Bodkin Farm near Shepshed, in Charnwood Forest. Her father managed a boot and shoe factory in Shepshed that had been established by Clare's grandfather. She recalled watching German zeppelins fly over her home in 1917 when they were bombing Loughborough.

She was taught at home by her mother and a governess; later the family returned to Leicester where Clare went to the Collegiate School. Girls with fathers in trade were looked down on by those in professions. The two headmistresses, Miss Jackson and Miss Thomas, taught the girls to stand on their own feet in a masculine world. The school split, with a day section remaining in Leicester with Miss Jackson and a boarding section going to Eastbourne with Miss Thomas. Clare went to Eastbourne, where girls changed for dinner, then danced in gym to latest jazz tunes. Finding herself to be too academic in a school where sport was the thing, she returned to Leicestershire where she attended Ashby Grammar School.

After leaving school, she got temporarily engaged to young man whose sole interests were the Territorials and the Hunt Ball. Clare had friends of all political persuasions, though she inclined to the left. She became interested in the League of Nations Union, and was appointed secretary to the LNU organiser for Worcestershire. However, a family friend, Frederick Attenborough, principal of Leicester University College and the father of Richard

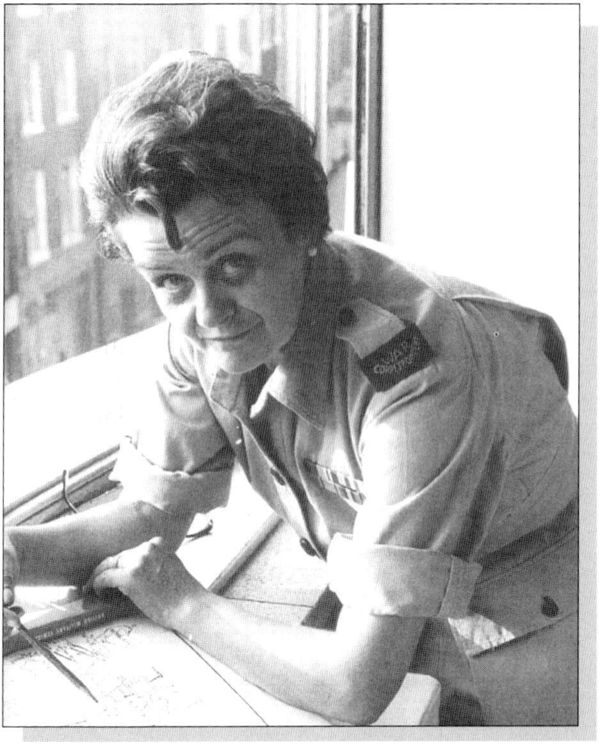

Clare Hollingworth at work

and David Attenborough, encouraged Clare to return to an academic life, and she obtained scholarship to the school of Slavonic Studies at London University. She then decided to take a course at Zagreb University, visiting Yugoslavia, Hungary, Bulgaria and Albania.

Clare broke with her fiancé, and met Vandeleur Robinson, the LNU organiser for the South East. They married at a registry office in London, then in a church in Leicester. Clare found her mother-in-law to be a great snob, and thought it amusing that she always signed her cheques in her full name: Ianthe-Bowes-Lyon Vandeleur Robinson.

Van and Clare both joined the Labour Party, and Clare returned to Leicester in 1937 to organise the Peace ballot. She saw Van at the weekends, and they spent their holidays travelling together in Eastern Europe until Hitler took over Austria and invaded the Sudetenland. Clare was appointed as the senior official based in Katovice, Poland, in the same building as the British Consulate, arranging for refugees (Jews, Catholics, Communists and Socialists) to travel to London.

Her parents accepted all this, and even Clare becoming a Labour Party parliamentary candidate, but were horrified when she said she would like to become a journalist. In August, Clare was taken on by the *Daily Telegraph* and immediately sent back to Poland. She landed in Warsaw and reported to the paper's correspondent there, Hugh Carleton Greene. Hugh said, 'One of us has to go to the German-Polish border,' and Clare replied that as she knew Katowice well, it would make sense for her to go to the border, while Hugh remained in Warsaw.

At Katowice, Clare notified John Anthony Thwaites, Consul General, that she was there to report for the *Telegraph*. Because there was no room in the hotels, she stayed in the Thwaites' flat. She found the atmosphere in Katowice cheerful and confident, the local Poles boasting that they would soon give those Germans a good hiding. The border with Germany had been closed, but it was open to cars with official flags, to enable Germans to get into Poland. Clare asked the Consul General if she could borrow his car (with its Union Jack flag). He asked where she wanted to go, and when she answered 'To Germany' he laughed in disbelief, but did allow her to borrow the car.

Clare immediately drove to the German border. There was some surprise at the border when a car flying the Union Jack arrived, but as their orders were to permit cars with official flags to pass, the German guards allowed her to cross into Germany. After buying some items, Clare headed back towards the border. As she was driving back through a valley she knew, she found that to her left a huge tarpaulin had been erected, so she couldn't see what was there. Suddenly, the tarpaulin blew away from its moorings, and behind it she saw scores of German tanks, ready to roll into Poland.

On her return, the Consul wouldn't believe she had managed to go into Germany until she showed him the newspapers she'd bought there. She then told him about the German troops and tanks that were lined up on the border, showing the exact position on his maps. The Consul contacted the Foreign Office, while Clare rang her *Telegraph* colleague in Warsaw with what should have been the scoop of the century. However, when her news reached the *Telegraph* in London, the news was not believed.

Two days later, Clare woke up to the sound of tanks rolling past. When she rang Warsaw to say that tanks were entering Poland, she was told that she was talking rubbish, as negotiations with Germany were still going on. Clare proved her point by putting the phone out of the window and letting Hugh Carleton Greene actually hear the sound of the tanks in Katowice. 'Yes you're right,' her colleague admitted grudgingly.

After escaping from Poland, Clare ended up in Rumania. She described one incident where thirty journalists were battling for the possession of the one public phone box to send their stories in. Clare was too small to fight her way through, so she crawled through the legs of the crowd and seized the phone.

Later she went to Egypt to report on the war in North Africa, but she came up against the prejudices of General Montgomery. 'Monty was something of a woman-hater,' she found, but she managed to stay on as a war correspondent by becoming accredited to the *Chicago Daily News*. As an

American correspondent, Monty had no powers to have her sent home.

After the Second World War, Clare Hollingworth travelled all over the world, always putting her career before domesticity. Her husband Van eventually divorced her on grounds of desertion, and Clare later married Geoffrey Hoare, a fellow journalist.

Clare never showed fear in a tight situation. During the Algerian war in the 1950s, she took action when an Italian journalist was seized from his hotel room by terrorists from the OAS, the extreme rightwing organisation dedicated to keeping Algeria under colonial rule. As the terrified man was about to be taken away to be shot, Clare rallied about eighty reporters to his aid. Outside the hotel, they surrounded the armed thugs, with Clare telling them that if they were taking in one reporter, they would have to take all eighty. The OAS backed off, and drove away empty-handed.

In January 1963 Clare obtained a real scoop, when she discovered that Kim Philby, long suspected of being the third man in the Burgess/Maclean spy case, had disappeared. Her story was, however, spiked by the *Guardian* editor, Alistair Hetherington, who described it as preposterous. A few months later, it was revealed that Philby had indeed defected and was living in Russia. Clare Hollingworth's scoop had been genuine.

In the years that followed, Clare travelled to every trouble spot in the world – Korea, India, Pakistan, Vietnam and China – becoming the leading woman correspondent on war and defence topics. In 1999 she appeared on the radio programme Desert Island Discs, and made a memorable contribution. As well as talking about her life and career, her choice of records included three national anthems (German, French and Chinese) as well as *Land of Hope and Glory* and *A Nightingale Sang in Berkeley Square*.

In February 2000 Clare, who was an early pioneer in the area of women war correspondents – a generation before Kate Adey

– was awarded a lifetime achievement award at the annual 'What The Papers Say' awards held at the Savoy Hotel. She was called the 'doyenne of war correspondents' whose career 'reads like a history of conflict in the twentieth century'. Always fascinated by the tactics and strategy of war, she explained, 'I enjoy action. I enjoy being in a plane that's bombing something on the ground in the desert when they're advancing.' Clare was never frightened by sound of shot and shell, but has admitted to being scared when entering a lift – having to take a deep breath before getting in!

While researching the exploits of Clare Hollingworth, who eventually retired to live in Switzerland, I was surprised to find nothing at all about this remarkable journalist in Loughborough library – the old saying about a prophet never being recognised in his own country comes to mind.

8

Thomas Cook

– pioneer of the travel industry

Early in his working life, although a wood-turner by profession, Thomas Cook was employed for five years by Joseph Winks, a Loughborough printer and publisher of religious pamphlets for the General Baptist Association. Thomas's religion, together with his love of travel and his advocacy of teetotalism, was a life-long commitment. He became a Village Missionary for the Baptist Church, with recorded visits to the town of Hinckley and the Leicestershire villages of Barton-in-the-Beans, Cossington, Billesdon, Measham, Nailstone and Ibstock. Many of his preaching tours were on foot and in one year, 1829, he walked over 2,100 miles in his evangelical work.

However, by 1832 funds were low and he went back to his woodworking profession, setting up in Market Harborough, making wooden toys and Windsor chairs. The following year he married Marianne Mason, a Rutland girl, and the young couple set up home in Adam and Eve Street. Their eldest son, Thomas Mason Cook, was born in January 1834. Thomas Cook actually became a total abstainer from alcohol in 1836, at the age of 28, when with six other men from the town he set up a local Temperance Society, becoming its secretary. The first meeting was held in the home of William Symington, a Market Harborough coffee and tea merchant, who became the society's president. For the rest of his life, Thomas Cook preached the benefits of temperance, and like other abstainers, he was often verbally and physically abused for his views. More than once, the Cooks' house had its windows stoned by those who disagreed with him.

THOMAS COOK

It was on a 15-mile journey – on foot, of course – to preach at a meeting in Leicester that Thomas Cook had a sudden brilliant idea. What a glorious thing it would be if the newly developed powers of railways and locomotion could be harnessed to the promotion of temperance. He put this strange notion to the Leicester meeting, gained support, and organised the first Thomas Cook excursion in July 1841. He hired a train to take supporters from Leicester on a trip to Loughborough. The fare of one shilling per head included not only the return fare, but also a picnic of tea and buns in a Loughborough park, and the services of a brass band while they ate. The whole enterprise was a huge success; 485 passengers made the journey, and more supporters joined them in Loughborough. After the picnic, games were played – cricket and tag – and these were followed by a mass meeting with sermons on the evils of alcohol. The Leicester travellers got back to Leicester station at 10.30 pm, tired but sober and happy. The day trip had been invented.

Soon afterwards, the Cook family moved to King Street, Leicester, and Thomas became a bookseller and stationer. He also became a publisher, and began his annual *Leicestershire Almanack, Directory, Guide to Leicester and Advertiser* – in the 1840s titles were long and explanatory rather than short and snappy. Thomas was delighted when John Briggs, a major Leicestershire hosiery manufacturer, put his warehouse at the disposal of the temperance movement, and he was able to organise a 'tea meeting' in the warehouse for a thousand supporters. Thomas Cook, now secretary of the Leicester Temperance Society, was making some influential friends. In 1853 he was able to open a Temperance Hall, and next door to it a Temperance Hotel, in Granby Street, Leicester, both situated somewhat ironically between two non-temperance public houses!

He continued to organise outings for local Sunday schools. In one, 300 children were taken by train to Syston; after a two-mile walk, they had a picnic and a service, before being transported back to Leicester. During race week, a time of temptation for many, Thomas took 3,000 children to Derbyshire, to keep them out of mischief.

Not all the excursions were by train. He took one party in nine horse-drawn carriages, to Pugin's Mount St Bernard's Abbey, near Whitwick in north-west Leicestershire, then over the Derbyshire border to Melbourne Hall. He also arranged with the Duke of Rutland to receive another party, again transported by horse-drawn carriages, at Belvoir Castle in the north-east of the county. In June 1850 Thomas arranged a train excursion to Ashby-de-la-Zouch, which included visits to Ivanhoe Baths, the Royal Hotel and the pleasure grounds to listen to music from two brass bands. The return fare of three shillings and sixpence (two shillings and sixpence in the cheaper carriages) did not include the meal at the Royal (another shilling), sampling the waters (sixpence) or an extra visit by carriage to Coleorton Hall (again sixpence).

The following year, Thomas Cook's excursions included Chatsworth House, Matlock and the Great Exhibition in London. The latter included the travellers staying in lodgings in London, so the day trip was expanding into something more. The Great Exhibition was a tremendous impetus to Thomas Cook's business, and over a period of six months, he conveyed 165,000 visitors to London.

He began to venture into trips abroad: to Ireland in1853, to the battlefield of Waterloo in 1855, then to Switzerland and Italy. By 1866 he had arranged his first tour of the USA, taking in Civil War battlefields, and three years later excursions to Egypt and to the Holy Land. In 1872 he organised his first round-the-world tour with nine companions. They sailed the Atlantic, visited New

The statue of Thomas Cook at Leicester railway station

York, Niagara Falls, Chicago, Salt Lake City and San Francisco, sailed to Yokohama, then took in Shanghai, Singapore, Ceylon and India, continuing through the Suez Canal to Turkey, Greece and finally back to England. The whole trip took 222 days, and was the beginning of the Thomas Cook world cruise.

Thomas opened an office in London, with young Thomas in charge, and made his son a partner in the firm. Thomas Cook & Son had been founded. Thomas senior retired in 1878 at the age of 70, and lived with his wife and daughter in a large house called

Thorncroft in Leicester's London Road. He died in 1892, and was buried in the Welford Road cemetery. The Prime Minister, William Gladstone, paid a tribute to Cook and his achievements, saying, 'Among the humanising contrivances of the age, I think notice is due to the system founded by Mr Cook, and now largely in use, under which numbers of persons, and indeed whole classes, have for the first time found easy access to foreign countries, and have acquired some of that familiarity with them, which breeds not contempt but kindness.' Allowing for the verbosity of the PM – soundbites were not in fashion in the 19th century – the words do give some indication of what Thomas Cook brought to ordinary people.

There are many plaques and memorials to Thomas Cook in Leicester, Loughborough and his native Melbourne, including a splendid bronze statue outside Leicester railway station. This monument was commissioned jointly by Leicester City Council, Thomas Cook International Ltd and British Rail and was unveiled in 1994 by another Thomas Cook, the pioneer's great-great-grandson. However, perhaps Thomas Cook's finest memorial is the travel firm that still bears his name.

9

Lady Florence Dixie

– intrepid traveller and champion of good causes

Florence Caroline Douglas married Sir Beaumont Dixie of Bosworth Park in 1875 when she was twenty. She was the daughter of the seventh Marquis of Queensbury, though her father had died when she was just three years old. When she was ten, her eldest brother Francis was killed on the Matterhorn while taking part in Edward Whymper's expedition.

Florence was an odd mixture of tomboy and romantic. As a girl she swam and rode untrained horses, sitting astride her horse when the normal ladylike method was to ride side-saddle. She would often dress in her twin brother's clothes, and pretend to be him. She caused a shock at court when she was presented to Queen Victoria while wearing her hair in a short bob, for which she was reprimanded by the Lord Chamberlain.

After her marriage she did her duty by providing her husband with the required two sons – an heir and a spare – then devoted the rest of her life to travel and adventures. When she was 23, she set off for South America. She was accompanied by her two brothers – John Sholto and her twin James – and her husband, although the organising and arrangements were done by Florence. The travelling was all on horseback, and for this Florence always wore a man's coat and hat and she still insisted on riding astride her horse. The expedition members lived in tents, and dined on the animals they hunted: ostriches, guanaco, geese and ducks.

On her return to Bosworth Hall, she wrote a book about the journey, *Across Patagonia*. She also brought back to Leicestershire a puma-skin rug and a live jaguar she called 'Affums'. She would alarm the local populace by taking Affums for walks on a lead in Bosworth Park. She also took her pet on a visit to Windsor, but Affums escaped and devoured several of the Queen's deer in Windsor Park. After much persuasion, Florence reluctantly agreed to donate her jaguar to London Zoo.

Her next adventure was to the USA. Although she travelled from the east side right across to California, Florence found North America too tame for her taste, compared to Patagonia. She was intending to head for Alaska and then to cross the Bering Strait for the wilds of what she called Tuski Land. However, she didn't complete that journey, because the *Birmingham Morning Post* asked her to become its special correspondent in the Transvaal, reporting on the war with the Boers. In Africa, she caused some comment by dressing in a plain serge suit. The criticisms didn't worry Florence, though she did say that she felt like a ruffian, compared with the ladies in their evening dresses she met while dining out in Kimberley. Florence had different skills from most of the other British ladies there. She was an excellent horsewoman, a first class shot, she knew how to bivouac in the wild, and, while in company, proved that she could play cricket and billiards as well as any man.

While she was in southern Africa, Florence went to Zululand where she met and interviewed the captured Cetschweyo, the Zulu King. After talking to him, Florence became an ardent champion of his cause, and wrote many newspaper articles, arguing that he should be restored to his throne. Her advocacy on behalf of Cetschweyo did not go down well in some quarters, and she made many enemies. One of them wrote that one of southern Africa's worst misfortunes was the visit of Lady Florence Dixie. However, Florence was a spirited and determined lady and her articles led to Cetschweyo being invited to London to meet Queen Victoria. When he was restored to his kingdom,

Cetschweyo said to Florence, 'Although you are a woman, you have beaten all the men in your talking for me.'

When Florence came back to Leicestershire, she had changed from being a relatively conventional believer in British imperialism to a champion of liberal and feminist causes. Despite having been brought up in the hunting tradition and having taken part in both stag and foxhunting – she met her husband Beau at a meet – Florence now became convinced the all bloodsports were cruel and unnecessary. As with every cause she took up, Florence argued her case with passion and determination. In her next book, *The Horrors of Sport*, she wrote, 'I regard with absolute loathing and detestation any sort of sport which is produced by the suffering of animals.'

She also championed equality between the sexes, and argued that all titles, including the monarchy, should pass to the firstborn child of either sex, rather than to the eldest son. She upset the writer Rider Haggard by saying that the heroines of his novels had to hide their natural talents in order that men alone should rule. Haggard responded by calling Florence a proto-suffragette, which he obviously meant as an insult.

Another cause taken up by Lady Florence Dixie was home rule for Ireland, though she did quarrel with the methods advocated by the Irish Land League. This disagreement was the probable cause of an incident in 1883 when Florence was attacked by two would-be assassins armed with knives. They managed to approach her disguised in women's clothes, then tried to stab her to death. A woman like Florence Dixie is not killed without putting up a struggle and she fought them off, suffering only a hand wound, although her clothing was slashed in several places.

As well as her travel books, Lady Florence Dixie also wrote two novels, *Redeemed in Blood* (1880) and a novel set in the future called *Gloriana: or the Revolution of 1900*, which was published in 1890. Under the pseudonym 'Darling', she published a collection of rather sentimental verses, *The Songs of a Child*, but it is as an intrepid adventurer and a champion of good causes that she is remembered.

Her husband Beau always loyally supported his spirited wife, though he did have outside interests of his own, particularly gambling. Because of his debts, he was forced to sell Bosworth Park, and he and Florence moved to Scotland, where she continued her writing and campaigning, despite being confined to a wheelchair through arthritis. She died in 1905.

10

Gary Lineker

– outstanding footballer and popular broadcaster

Gary Lineker was born in Leicester on 30th November 1960, the son of well-known Leicester market traders. The Lineker fruit and veg stall is a famous Leicester landmark, and since Gary's rise to fame, the object of veneration for visiting sports fans. Gary's middle name, Winston, is due to him being born on Winston Churchill's birthday.

Gary's final school report stated that he 'must devote less of his time to sport if he wants to be a success', which must go down in history of one of the least insightful of pedagogic prophecies. He had trained with Leicester City from the age of thirteen, and three years later he signed up and began to play full-time for the club. Initially, he was used as a winger, playing wide, but eventually it became obvious that his ball-control and dribbling skills might be better employed as a striker. He was always alert to any goal-scoring chance and began to be recognised throughout the football world as a player who could put the ball in the net. His critics called him a predatory goal poacher, but even they have to admit that every team needs someone to actually score goals. It's all very well creating chances but it is the team with a goal-scoring striker that actually wins matches.

Inevitably, and in spite of his club being a comparatively lowly one, Gary was selected to play for England and between 1984 and 1992 he made eighty appearances for the national side, becoming the England team captain from 1990. His 48 goals make him England's second-highest scorer, second only to Sir Bobby Charlton.

Gary Lineker

Gary spent eight years at Leicester City before moving on to Everton, Barcelona (Terry Venables signed him for £2,750,000 in 1986), Spurs and then a team called Grampus Eight in Japan. Gary has many claims to fame, as well as his quicksilver goal-scoring qualities. For me, the most impressive is that throughout his career, at international and at club level, he was never once cautioned by any referee. He never had a yellow card, let alone a red. This is due to his placid temperament, his ability to control a football and his skill as a dribbler. Cynics always add '... and his inability to tackle', but the truth is that his card-free career is down to the fact that he was a good-natured player, who didn't need to foul his opponents to win. His attitude to the game led to him gaining the FIFA Fair Play Award in 1990. This recognition can be added to his PFA Footballer of the Year and runner-up European Footballer of the Year titles in 1986, and the Football Writers' Association Player of the Year title in both 1986 and 1992. In the 1986 World Cup he was presented with the Golden Boot, as the top scorer in the whole competition.

Despite his lack of academic success as a schoolboy, he has honorary MA degrees from both Loughborough and Leicester Universities, and was made an OBE in 1992. In that same year, he was made an honorary Freeman of the City of Leicester, joining Earl Haig (1922), Ramsay MacDonald (1929), David and Richard Attenborough (1990) and Alec Jeffreys (1992). To be given the Freedom of Leicester, the nomination must be conferred at a special meeting of the City Council, after a resolution passed by a two-thirds majority. In the case of Gary Lineker, the resolution was passed unanimously. His citation stated that he was made a Freeman of Leicester in recognition and appreciation of the honour and distinction brought to the City by virtue of his contribution to football at national and international level and his outstanding sportsmanship.

Gary married his childhood sweetheart Michelle in Leicester, and the couple have four sons. Their oldest, George, was diagnosed with leukaemia but is now fully recovered. Research into childhood leukaemia is one of the many charities that Gary espouses. He also continues to support Leicester City. When the Foxes were in trouble, going into administration, it was Gary Lineker who put together a consortium to rescue his old club. The consortium included Emile Hesky, another Foxes old boy who was born and bred in Leicester, among its number.

Gary on the field (courtesy of the *Leicester Mercury*)

When Gary retired from playing football in 1994, following a toe injury, he went into broadcasting and newspaper journalism. He is a well-known figure on television, commentating on football matches and compèring sports programmes. His likeable manner, together with his famous ears and that unmistakable Leicester accent, make him a popular presenter. *Match of the Day* is not his only television show. To counter his squeaky clean image, he appears as a regular team captain on the laddish *They Think It's All Over*, striving – with only limited success – to appear as rude as the other performers: Jonathan Ross, Rory McGrath, David Seaman, Phil Tuffnell, Nick Hancock etc. At one time, the two team captains were Gary Lineker and cricketer David Gower, another Leicestershire sportsman.

The Leicester firm of Walkers also use Gary as a regular star in their television advertisements for crisps. Again they amusingly counteract his goody-goody image by making him portray ultra mean and menacing characters, a punk, a headmistress, the devil, always playing against type and trying to steal crisps from innocent children.

When Leicester City's former ground in Filbert Street was demolished and apartment blocks built on the site, there was a public vote on the name of the new street. Not surprisingly, it is called Lineker Road. Gary has received many honours and awards as a sportsman, but one of them is unique. How many footballers are named in the title of a successful play? Just one: Gary Lineker. *An Evening With Gary Lineker*, written by Arthur Smith and Chris England, has the characters watching England's semi-final against Germany in the 1990 World Cup. As the match switches between the characters watching the television and the actual match, one of them, Monica, dreams of having an affair with Gary Lineker, whom she memorably describes as 'the Queen Mother of football'. The honour of having a play with your name in the title must surely rank along with an honorary MA, a player of the year award, or even an OBE.

11

Philip Bent

– recipient of a posthumous VC for bravery at Passchendaele

Philip Eric Bent was a student at Ashby-de-la-Zouch Boys' Grammar School in Leicestershire from 1907 until 1911. When he left school he went into the merchant navy, gaining his Second Mate's ticket in early 1914. He was ashore when war broke out and enlisted on 2nd October 1914. For some inexplicable reason he joined the Army rather than the Royal Navy, and he became a private in the Royal Scots regiment. He did not stay a private for long, as in November he was given a commission as a temporary second lieutenant in the Leicestershire regiment known as 'The Tigers'. His rise through the ranks was incredible. By August 1915, when he sailed to France, he was a full lieutenant, and the following April he was a temporary captain. In August 1916, he was a major, second in command of his battalion, and was then promoted further. At the age of 25, Philip Bent was the youngest soldier to ever reach the rank of Lieutenant Colonel.

He had seen earlier action at the Battle of the Somme, where he was wounded. His leadership, described as superb, was recognised in June 1917 when he was awarded the DSO. Interestingly his rank at that time was recorded as Second Lieutenant, Temporary Major and Acting Lieutenant Colonel. Four months later, Philip met his death – and won his Victoria Cross – at Passchendaele. At 5.25 am on 1st October, The Tigers came under an enemy barrage and the Germans attacked through a smoke screen. Initially driven off, the enemy attacked again and were this time successful. In the face of German flame throwers, artillery and grenades, Lt Col Philip Bent personally led a platoon in a rifle and bayonet counter-attack. The Germans retreated, but Philip Bent was killed.

The following January he was awarded a posthumous VC. His citation said that the award was: *For most conspicuous bravery, when during a heavy hostile attack, the right of his command and the battalion on his right were forced back. The situation was critical owing to the confusion caused by the attack and the intense artillery fire. Lieutenant Colonel Bent personally collected a platoon which was in reserve, and together with men from other companies and various regimental details, he organised and led them forward to the counter-attack, after issuing orders to other officers as to the further defence of the line. The counter-attack was successful, and the enemy was checked. The coolness and magnificent example shown to all ranks by Lieutenant Colonel Bent resulted in the securing of a portion of the line which was of essential importance for subsequent operations. This very gallant officer was killed whilst leading a charge which he inspired with the call of 'Come on, the Tigers'.*

In 1923 Philip Bent's mother sent his VC to Ashby Grammar School to 'inspire and encourage future generations'. In 1972 the medal was presented to the Leicestershire Regimental Museum in Leicester on permanent loan. In 2004 the school made a twelve-minute film about their heroic ex-student and a replica VC was put on display. The school is rightly proud of its hero, and of a former master at the school, Colonel Bernard Vann, who was also given a posthumous VC after being killed while leading a charge just before the end of the same war. 'It is remarkable', a school spokesman said, 'that two Victoria Crosses should have been won by people from this school.'

12

Sue Townsend

– the creator of Adrian Mole

Sue was born in 1946 in a prefab off Hillsborough Road in the south of Leicester, and she remembers spending her pre-school childhood summers playing in the dust of potholes in the unfinished roads, making mudpies. In winter she and her playmates would dam the brooklets that ran down the roads. They played in the nearby fields and woods, collecting conkers in autumn and picking wildflowers in spring. It was a time of freedom and joy.

In 1951 she started school, which she describes as 'a descent into Hell'. Her school, Glen Hills Primary, was situated in a middle-class area to the west of the main Lutterworth Road, and she was forced to wear a uniform – gymslip, white shirt with stiff collar and tie – which she didn't enjoy. She met for the first time the English class system; children from the nice houses were advised by their parents not to play with those children from the prefabs on the far side of the main road. Sue was literally from the wrong side of the track, or rather the A426.

Although Sue didn't enjoy her time at the school – she mentions the frequent slaps on the leg and learning to read Janet and John books by pointing to each word and chanting it in unison – her eldest granddaughter Gabrielle recently attended the same school and found it a place of delight. Some things have obviously changed for the better since the 1950s. Another difference is that Sue tried to avoid school assemblies by picking flowers for the dinner hall. In her own words, 'It meant I missed

Sue Townsend

the religious assembly, but I didn't mind that, I was getting tired of pretending to believe in God.' Gabrielle, on the other hand, has become a fervent believer.

There is just one thing Sue remembers with pleasure from her time at Glen Hills Primary, a teacher, Mr Moles, who introduced her to comic literature. 'He would read to us until tears of laughter ran down his face,' she recalls, 'and we children were weak with laughter.' I wonder if that teacher ever realised just what seeds of comic genius he was sowing in one of his young listeners! I am sure that this inspirational teacher can be

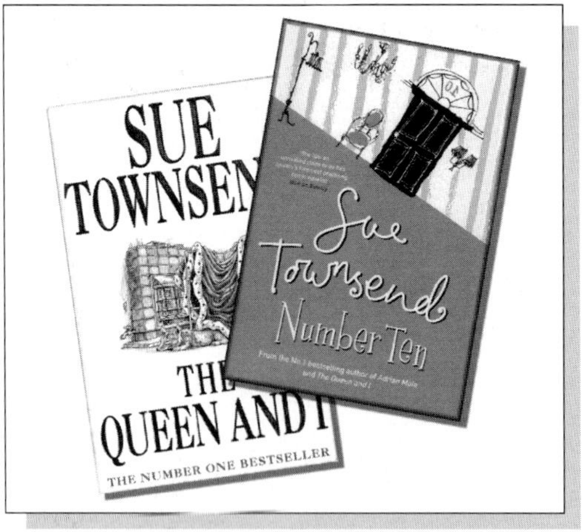

seen in Mr Newman, a character who appears in one of Sue's novels.

Sue went on to South Wigston Secondary Modern School for Girls where again she did not shine academically. She did, however, discover Russian literature and devoured the novels of Dostoyevsky and Tolstoy avidly. Sue left school at fifteen and had a variety of jobs including becoming a petrol pump attendant, a factory worker and a supervisor of a children's adventure playground. She married at eighteen, but this teenage marriage did not last. She later married Colin Broadway, a canoe builder, with whom she has lived happily ever since.

Colin talked her into attending a playwriting course, where Sue sat quietly at the back. It was only when they had to write a piece of their own that the tutors discovered her talent. It is not always realised that Sue Townsend is a successful playwright, as well as a renowned novelist. She became resident playwright at the Leicester Phoenix Theatre in 1978, and in the early 1980s she won the Thames TV playwright award. Her plays include *Bazaar and Rummage*, *Groping For Words*, *The Queen and I*, and

Womberang (where a group of pregnant women forced to queue in at a health centre rebel against the bureaucrats, take over the waiting room and organise it in a more humane fashion).

Sue adapted the play *The Queen and I* from her novel of the same name. This richly hilarious book, set in 1992, describes how a newly elected republican government deposes the royal family. They come to live on a Leicester council estate in neighbouring houses in Hellebore Close, usually abbreviated to Hell Close, and for the first time come into contact with real life and real people. As the Queen and her husband quarrel over whether they are to be known as Mr and Mrs Windsor or Mountbatten, Charles decides to adopt the maiden name of his great-grandmother and becomes Charlie Teck.

The Queen Mum is shocked to discover that one has to *buy* toilet paper – it is not automatically provided – while her son-in-law learns how to shave himself. The Queen cuts herself opening a tin of corned beef and has to be taken by her son to a long wait in A&E at the local hospital. Harris, the Queen's dog causes some concern when he runs with the feral pack of estate dogs and Diana has similar problems with William and Harry.

Although *The Queen and I* does find humour in the plight of the royals, it is not mean-spirited or unsympathetic. The Queen generously gives her own clean sheets and the loan of a silver kettle when she assists at the birth of a neighbour's baby, and finds great satisfaction in being able to help. The Queen Mum makes friends with her elderly black neighbour, who is very anti drinking and gambling, but whose son is helpful in taking the Queen Mum's betting slips to his bookie. And who can ever forget the wonderfully comic scene in the DSS office, when the Queen attempts to get an emergency payment. She is getting absolutely nowhere until she has a stroke of genius, calling out that her dog is starving. The dog-loving DSS clerk gives her £3 to buy dog food, which she immediately diverts to buy food for the family.

Another of Sue's novels *Rebuilding Coventry* tells how a Leicester woman – Coventry Dakin – runs away from home in a state of panic after killing a neighbour's abusive husband by hitting him on the back of the neck with a toy action man. Typical Sue Townsend black surreal humour. The first chapter ends: 'Yesterday, I had a husband and two teenage children. Today, I am alone, I'm on the run, I'm in London, *without my handbag*.' What a wonderfully telling phrase! I am reliably informed by the women in my family that those final three words do convey convincingly the state that Coventry Dakin was in.

In 2002 Sue wrote *Number Ten*, a satirical story about prime minister Edward Clare and his wife Adele Floret-Clare, said to be the cleverest woman in Europe. Edward, although voted in with a landslide victory, is losing his popular appeal and ends up travelling round the country incognito with his policeman friend Jack Sprat, the bobby who normally stands outside 10 Downing Street. Not surprisingly, they find their way to the Leicester home of PC Sprat's mother. Sue denies, with varying degrees of conviction, that Edward and Adele Clare are really Tony and Cherie Blair. She does admit to surprise that people found the book vicious, adding that she thought she had in fact watered down what things were really like in everyday life.

Although Sue Townsend is rightly admired for her witty plays and radical novels, she is best known, of course, for her creation of Adrian Mole. In a series of books, Sue traces the longings and setbacks of the legendary Adrian as revealed in his diaries. Sue chose the diary format partly because it is a way of showing the diarist's innermost thoughts, but she also remembered reading the diaries of Leicester writers Joe Orton and Colin Wilson, written when they were about twelve years old.

SUE TOWNSEND

The first Mole book, *The Secret Diary of Adrian Mole Aged 13¾*, was an immediate success. Adrian's adolescent yearnings for the beautiful but unavailable Pandora Braithwaite, his literary ambitions, and his problems with his family combined to make this book a witty and comic bestseller. In later books, Adrian lives in Ashby-de-la-Zouch, a town where the local MP is his beloved Pandora. I sometimes wonder if I played a part in this! Soon after the first Adrian Mole book was published, I collected Sue Townsend from her Leicester home and brought her to Ashby to talk to the local Writers' Club. It was the first time she had visited the town, so did I give the idea of using Ashby in later Mole books? I would like to think so. The Adrian Mole diaries have been translated into 42 languages and have sold over ten million copies.

Sue is now both wheelchair bound and virtually blind, the latter condition caused by diabetic retinopathy and cataracts, the former by a form of degenerative arthritis called Charcot's joint. The little sight she has left does enable her to work at a greatly magnified computer screen but the strain involved means she can do it for only for fifteen minutes at a time. Her books are now dictated to her husband Colin, who types them into the computer and then reads her work back again. She does miss being able to read, but listens to audio books and to books read to her by Colin and the family.

Colin also paints her nails and chooses her lipstick but for the selection of her outfits she enlists the help of her daughters. She manages to put on her own makeup but does ask her husband to do a 'Coco-check' before she goes out, to make sure she doesn't look like the famous clown. At the Women of the Year lunch in October 2003, Sue Townsend was presented with the Frink award for achievement in the face of adversity. Sue continues to live in Leicester and has four children and seven grandchildren, one of whom has, at nine years old, begun to write short stories and plays. Sue is delighted.

13

David and Richard Attenborough

– Leicester brothers known throughout the world for their work in TV and film

Frederick Attenborough, the son of a village baker, was the principal of Leicester University College from 1932 until 1952. The institution was called a University College because in the early days it did not award degrees of its own but those from London University. Freddie, as he was always known, loved art and music and passed on his appreciation of these to his sons. As a youth he'd had ambitions to be a footballer, but a badly set broken leg ended that particular dream. With his wife Mary, he worked to get Basque refugee children brought over to Evington Hall during the Spanish Civil War, and later helped to bring Jewish children out of Germany. Freddie Attenborough was a well-known and well-loved figure in Leicester, often seen driving his distinctive brown and cream Humber car. When Professor W.H. ' Billie' Hoskins was writing his books about local history, Freddie, his principal, was usually his combined chauffeur and photographer.

Freddie's sons attended the nearby Wyggeston Grammar School for Boys and two of them – David and Richard – went on to make a name for themselves. After service in the Royal Navy, and three years as an editorial assistant at a firm that published educational books, David joined the BBC as a trainee producer in 1952. The series *Zoo Quest* enabled him to travel the world,

Richard and David Attenborough (courtesy of the *Leicester Mercury*)

capturing on film images of wildlife in its natural habitat, often in very remote locations.

David had actually begun his love affair with the world of Nature while hunting for snakes and other creatures in Charnwood Forest and Bradgate Park. In 1965 he was controller of BBC2, and introduced colour television into the UK. He then became Director of Programmes with editorial responsibility for both BBC1 and 2, before returning to his first love, making wildlife documentaries. He went on to make a number of memorable BBC series, including *Life on Earth*, *The Life of Birds*, *The Life of Mammals*, *The Private Life of Plants* and *The Trials of Life*. *Life on Earth*, which David both wrote and presented, was sold to a hundred countries and is estimated to have been watched by 500 million people worldwide. Who can ever forget that wonderful sequence as he sat murmuring to – and being groomed by – an enormous female gorilla? Our attitude to gorillas has never been the same since, and neither has our admiration for David Attenborough. His common touch, explaining zoological and environmental science in a way that is accessible to everyone, has made him one of the country's best television performers and producers.

David Attenborough, a trustee of the Royal Society and Kew Gardens and president of the Royal Society for Nature Conservation, was knighted in 1985. Molly Badham, the owner of Leicestershire's Twycross Zoo, told a local newspaper that Sir David has had a huge impact in stimulating interest in different creatures and promoting conservation. 'I don't think Twycross would have done so well without him. He made everyone want to come and visit the animals they had seen on television.'

David's elder brother Richard went into acting. The whole Attenborough family was involved with Leicester's Little Theatre, and his first scriptwriting venture is said to have been a sketch called *Ladies Wot Come To Oblige* put on by the 9th Leicester Cubs and starring both Richard and David. Richard's stage ambitions must have led to him neglecting his schoolwork as one of his reports from Wyggeston School stated baldly that his academic application was 'Nil'.

However, Richard got a scholarship to RADA in 1941 and his professional acting career had begun. His first film part came in 1942 when he played a frightened young sailor in the war film *In Which We Serve*, but one early unforgettable role was that of Pinkie, a sadistic and vicious young gangster, in the play, and later the film, *Brighton Rock*. He became a regular actor in over fifty films, playing characters as varied as the bombastic sergeant-major in *Guns at Batasi*, the jolly bearded Santa Claus in the remake of *Miracle on 34th Street*, and the sinister murderer John Christie in *10 Rillington Place*. A new generation of filmgoers will remember him as the millionaire John Hammond in *Jurassic Park*.

Richard later became a brilliant film director, notably of *Shadowlands*, *Cry Freedom*, which told the story of anti-apartheid hero Steve Biko, *Chaplin*, *Young Winston*, *A Bridge Too Far* and the multi-Oscar winning *Gandhi*, a film he worked to get on the screen for over twenty years. With writer Bryan Forbes, Richard set up the successful production company Beaver Films.

Richard Attenborough, who has been married to actress Sheila Sim since 1945, was knighted in 1976 and became a life peer in 1994. He still takes a keen interest in his boyhood home of Leicester. He is a life vice-president of the Little Theatre, and the patron of Leicester's Attenborough Centre for Disability and the Arts. He is also president of several national institutions: RADA, BAFTA, the Muscular Dystrophy Group of Great Britain and the Gandhi Foundation.

Richard Attenborough has remembered Leicester in other ways too. In 2003, Leicester City Museums made a dramatic announcement. An anonymous benefactor had donated a large number of original Picasso ceramics on permanent loan. (No, Picasso wasn't just a painter. He created many plates and sculptured pots in his studio in southern France.) The source of the wonderful gift of 144 pieces was tracked down in April 2004, and proved to be Lord and Lady Attenborough, who had spent fifty years assembling the collection. The exhibition in New Walk Museum and Art Gallery is to be called The Hand of Picasso, and is an exhibition of national importance that will draw lovers of Picasso's work from all over the world to Leicester. Some London-based critics were frankly 'sniffy' about the exhibition being based outside the capital, but others were more generous. Rebecca Wilson, editor of *Art Review*, said, 'It's fantastic that work of this quality is being shown outside London.' In Leicester the news was greeted with more enthusiasm, with comments from local artists like 'I don't know how they pulled it off. It's amazing,' and 'It is terrific. We don't really get a lot of top-class stuff coming to Leicester.'

Leicester, the city where Richard and David Attenborough grew up will always remember with pride two of its favourite heroes.

14

George Fox

– founder of the Quaker movement

Today the Quakers, more correctly known as the Society of Friends, have adherents in sixty-four countries, including 19,000 in the UK and 210,000 in the USA. They have no set creed or ceremonies, and believe that there is "that of God" in every human being. The movement was founded in the seventeenth century, where it was regarded as revolutionary because of its members' refusal to recognise any class distinctions, to swear any oaths to the authorities, to pay tithes, to adopt any sacraments or to accept any set ministry. From its beginning, it recognised complete sexual equality in worship. Many great reformers – including Elizabeth Fry – came from within the Quaker movement. Because of their belief in listening to their conscience – the God within – rather than to outside authorities, many Quakers are also pacifists.

George Fox was born in 1624 at Fenny Drayton, then known as Drayton-in-the Clay, in south-west Leicestershire. The son of a weaver, he was baptised in the local Anglican church like his brothers and sisters, but from an early age he took his religion very seriously. His questions and his reasoning on matters of divinity astonished the villagers, and his thoughts were said to be 'beyond his years'.

As a young man he was apprenticed to a shoemaker, but he found that his deeply religious and puritan outlook was not shared by either the church into which he had been baptised or by society in general. Everywhere he came across what he termed 'wantonness'. At the age of nineteen he obeyed what he believed

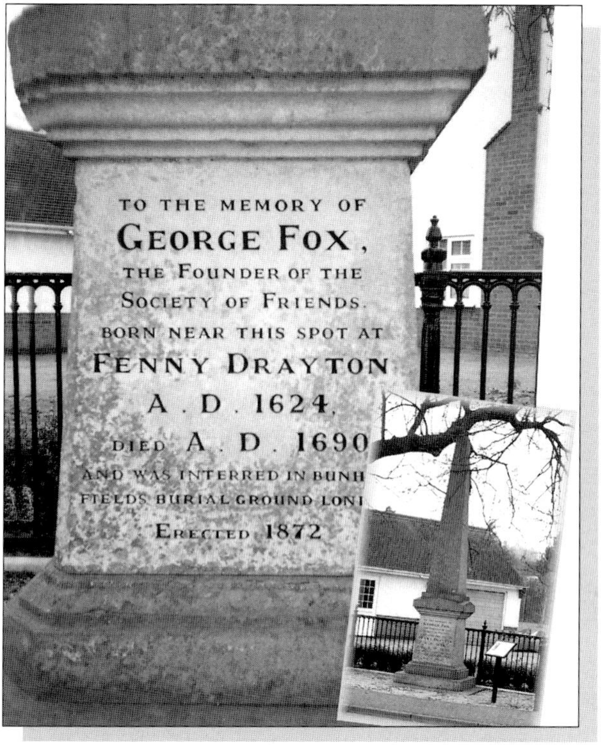
TO THE MEMORY OF
GEORGE FOX,
THE FOUNDER OF THE
SOCIETY OF FRIENDS.
BORN NEAR THIS SPOT AT
FENNY DRAYTON
A.D. 1624,
DIED A.D. 1690
ERECTED 1872

The monument to George Fox at Fenny Drayton

to be a divine call to 'forsake all, young and old, to keep out of the way of all, and be a stranger to all.' Abandoning his apprenticeship and the whole of his former life, he left home and wandered the land, Bible in hand, as an itinerant preacher.

Although he travelled all over the country, many of his significant events took place in Leicestershire. He preached his first outdoor sermon at Broughton Astley in 1647, in front of the village church. He always preferred to address meetings in the open air, rather than in what he called steeple-houses, the buildings of the established church. He did occasionally talk at indoor meetings and it was at one such gathering in Leicester, the following year, that he first used the phrase 'a society of friends' to describe his supporters. The Society of Friends is, of course, the correct term for the Quaker movement.

He became a famous – or, to the establishment, notorious – figure in his leather breeches and his wide-brimmed hat. He refused to take off his hat to anyone, as he recognised no master but God, and this did not endear him to the civil or religious authorities. He was imprisoned on eight occasions for denouncing capital punishment, the swearing of oaths and ministers of the church who were paid for their work. Another summons was for brawling in a 'steeple-house', though it was the churchgoers who actually started the fight when they objected to his presence. Although he had many followers, opponents often broke up his meetings. When he preached in the open air, he was heckled, beaten and even stoned by mobs of people who found his views unacceptable.

In 1650, when he was brought before a court in Derby on a charge of blasphemy, George Fox told the judge that he should 'quake at the name of the Lord', and the name Quakers became used to describe those who supported him. Initially it was used to mock them, but they soon adopted it themselves.

He travelled widely, throughout England, Scotland and Ireland. In 1671 he went to the West Indies and North America, where one of his supporters was William Penn who founded the state of Pennsylvania and the city of Philadelphia. Some years later he preached in Germany and Holland. Despite his nomadic lifestyle he did take a wife. In 1669 he married Margaret Fell, the daughter of a Lancashire judge. She had been an active member of the movement since 1652, approaching both Cromwell and, after the restoration of the monarchy, Charles II, asking for respect for the Quakers. Some 4,000 Quakers had been imprisoned when he came to the throne.

The Quakers did have some successes. In 1689, two years before the death of George Fox, the Toleration Act was passed. This recognised the strong views of the Society of Friends on the subject of swearing oaths on the Bible, and for the first time people were allowed to make an affirmation rather than swear an oath of allegiance.

In Fenny Drayton, a small monument in memory of the founder of the Society of Friends was erected in 1872. It stands at the corner of Old Forge Road and George Fox Lane.

15

Alec Jeffreys

– the inventor of DNA fingerprinting

In September 1984 Alec Jeffreys was a young geneticist doing research at Leicester University. He was studying the genetic coding of the proteins that carry oxygen in the muscles. Using blood samples from animals and also from Jenny Foxon, one of his lab technicians, and her parents, he ran an experiment to discover whether he could detect highly variable regions in DNA (deoxyribonucleic acid). The experiment was successful. But as Alec Jeffreys studied his results he realised in a blinding flash that they, in fact, showed much more. Those random and apparently useless bits of DNA contained in the genes were unique to each individual, but he could also identify kinship patterns. The implications were clear to him. As an offshoot of his main research into genetic markers, he had discovered repeated patterns of DNA that led to his invention of DNA fingerprinting. His eureka moment occurred, aptly, at nine o'clock on a Monday morning. It was the beginning of a new week and the start of a new age in forensic science.

Collaborating with the Home Office, he began to refine the technology. It was now possible to produce a barcode of dark bands on an X-ray film that was specific to each individual person. Only identical twins would have the same barcode; everyone else would have a DNA fingerprint that was unique.

Alec Jeffreys was made a fellow of the Royal Society in 1985, and he was awarded a full professorship at Leicester University. Although other scientists knew that his invention was genuine

Professor Alec Jeffreys

and fully reliable, sceptics in the legal profession, the police service and among the general public had still to be convinced.

Initial interest was focussed on the fact that half of an individual's DNA barcode was inherited from his father and half from his mother. This could prove invaluable in cases of disputed paternity. One of the first public applications of it came in a case where the British Immigration authorities were refusing to readmit a Ghanaian boy who wanted to return to live with his mother in England. The Home Office was disputing that the boy was genuinely her son. Alec Jeffreys employed his techniques, and tests on the DNA of blood samples from the boy and his mother immediately proved that the Ghanaian family was telling the truth. The Home Office had to admit their doubts about the boy's parentage were incorrect, and the family was reunited.

An even more dramatic application of DNA fingerprinting came in a Leicestershire murder case in nearby Narborough. A 15-year-old girl, Lynda Mann, had been raped and murdered in November 1983 but the police investigation had got nowhere. When another girl, Dawn Ashworth, was raped and murdered in a very similar manner in August 1986, the police were convinced that the same man had committed both crimes. After the second murder, they arrested a local 17-year-old youth who had been acting suspiciously. Following a series of interviews over a period of fifteen hours, during which the youth kept changing his story, he eventually agreed that he had killed Dawn Ashworth. Although he signed a confession to the second murder, he was adamant that he had not killed Lynda Mann three years earlier.

The police were convinced that the two crimes were by the same man. The method used by the rapist-murderer was identical in both cases, and both murders had taken place within a mile of one another. They decided to send samples of the killer's semen to Alec Jeffreys just five miles away in Leicester University, together with a blood sample from the boy under arrest, and ask him to use DNA fingerprinting to confirm their suspicion. To say that the results were startling would be an understatement. What Alec Jeffreys proved was that the two murders were indeed committed by the same man, but that it was not the youth under arrest. His confession was untrue. He was released, though a few officers were still suspicious, muttering about good old-fashioned police work being undermined by professors from the University.

The significance of this event was immediately apparent. Not only could Alec Jeffreys' invention prove guilt, it could also prove innocence.

In 1987 the Leicestershire police announced that they were going to use DNA fingerprinting in an unprecedented way. Every man living or working in the Narbough-Enderby-Littlethorpe area would be 'invited' to give a blood sample for comparison with the samples they already had from the killer. It was theoretically voluntary sample, but the pressure to volunteer when you got your invitation was overwhelming. Over 4,000 tests were made, but the murderer, Colin Pitchfork from Littlethorpe, panicked. He persuaded a workmate from Hampshire Bakery to go and give a sample in his place. The workmate eventually gossiped about this in a pub and the police were informed. Pitchfork was arrested, tried and sentenced to life imprisonment. In this case, the fear of genetic fingerprinting had been enough to solve the crime. It also had the effect of convincing the police, some of whom had been sceptical initially, that they now had a new tool in the fight against crime. Catching the real murderer had been achieved through old-fashioned police work *plus* the new science.

Since then, genetic fingerprinting has been used as a forensic tool in many thousands of cases. Although in the early days, a blood or saliva sample was needed, it is now possible to obtain a genetic code from the merest trace – a hair, a drop of sweat, a flake of skin, even a few microscopic cells – left at the scene of a crime. Samples taken in minor crimes have resulted in the solving of murders committed decades earlier. In 2001 Leicestershire police arrested Desford man Tony Jasinskyj for assaulting his wife. A routine DNA taken from him proved that he was responsible for the murder of a Hampshire schoolgirl, Marion Crofts, in 1981, a crime that had remained unsolved for twenty years.

Professor Jeffreys' invention has been used in more unusual

ways too – for example, to identify the body of Josef Mengele, the Nazi doctor, using samples from the doctor's wife and son. It has also been used to identify the remains of Tsar Nicholas II of Russia, executed in 1918. Recently, following the tragic tsunami in Southeast Asia, a baby boy, just 4 months old, was found alive in Sri Lanka. He was nicknamed 'Baby 81', as he was the 81st admission to the hospital on the day he was brought in. Nine families – each of which had lost a baby in the disaster – claimed the boy was theirs. It was Alec Jeffreys' invention that led to the real parents – Murugupillai and Jenita Jeyarajah – being identified and their young son, Abilass, being restored to them. Had it not been for genetic fingerprinting, the authorities would have had no means of deciding between the nine claimants, and the baby would have been brought up in care. Genetic fingerprinting was also used to prove that Dolly the sheep really was a clone, and that the captured Saddam Hussein was the genuine article. In 2002 DNA fingerprinting released an innocent man from Death Row in Arizona. Ray Krone had been found guilty of killing a barmaid in 1992, when a dental expert said bite marks on the dead girl were his. Eleven years later, DNA from saliva left in the bite marks proved that the dental expert was wrong and that Ray was innocent.

Genetic fingerprinting is now a huge international business, generating £1 billion per annum. A very small proportion of this goes to Professor Sir Alec Jeffreys. Most of the money goes to the Lister Institute, who were his employers in 1984 when he made his world-shaking discovery. Alec has expressed some disquiet about some aspects of genetic fingerprinting. Genetic profiles stored by the police record the details of ten specific parts of the chain of molecules that make up anyone's DNA, and the odds of any two people sharing the same ten markers is said to be a billion to one. However, Professor Jeffreys now considers that the number of profiles being held by the police, currently between two and three million in the UK, mean that fifteen or sixteen markers would be more foolproof, making a wrong identification virtually impossible.

He is also concerned about researchers who are trying to use his invention to determine a person's race and medical history from DNA samples. 'That is just not on,' he says. The problem is caused by the fact that only half the samples found at crime scenes match profiles being held by the police. In the UK, the police are only allowed to keep DNA profiles of people suspected of a crime although, surprisingly, they are able to retain this data even if the person is found not guilty by a court. Alec's solution is even more controversial. He believes that there should be a global database containing the DNA fingerprint of every man woman and child, though he thinks that information about race, medical health and physical appearance should be banned to prevent civil liberty abuses. 'We're all used to birth, death and marriage certificates,' he argues. 'Imagine an equivalent of Somerset House holding DNA profiles. It would give you protection as an individual, proving you are you.'

Sir Alec Jeffreys – he was knighted for his contribution to science in 1994 – continues to work in the Genetics Department at Leicester University, and this modest and very human figure can often be seen outside the buildings, smoking one of his home-made roll-ups. He still sports the beard he grew as a young man to conceal the burns he suffered as a boy when his chemistry set blew up in his face. Although he has been offered many financial inducements to leave Leicester University and work elsewhere, he has resisted them all. He says that he would rather work in the University lab than sit behind a desk to head up some vast organisation. His loyalty to Leicester is reciprocated. In a poll in the Leicester Mercury newspaper, Sir Alec Jeffreys came top in the list of local heroes, beating David and Richard Attenborough and even Gary Lineker.

16

Malcolm Pinnegar

– striking miner who steadfastly followed his conscience

Malcolm Pinnegar was the leader of a band of men known as the Dirty Thirty. During the 1984 coalminers' strike, many mining areas, including Yorkshire, Durham, South Wales, Kent and Scotland, had 100% support for the strike, but in Leicestershire, only 30 of the 2,500 miners came out. One who did was Malcolm Pinnegar.

Malcolm is Leicestershire born and bred, growing up in the village of Stoney Stanton. He went to the village school, then to Heathfield High School in Earl Shilton, finishing his schooldays in Burbage. He left school at fifteen, and went into engineering. He worked at Jones & Shipman, then at Bentley Engineering, where machines for the knitting industry were made. He became active in union affairs and was soon the shop steward for the men on the night shift. At Bentleys he learned a lot about wage negotiations, as well as standing up for his colleagues.

Later he moved to Imperial Typewriters, but in the early 1970s he became a coalminer at Bagworth pit. 'One Wednesday in the spring 1984,' he told me, 'I came up from working on the afternoon shift to find that Bagworth was being picketed by men from Kent.' The Thatcher government was trying to close down a number of Yorkshire pits. Yorkshire miners had gone on strike to defend their jobs, and other areas were supporting them. Kent was a militant area, because many of the men who went to work there had been activists who had been blacklisted from their own areas. 'At first,' Malcolm says with a chuckle, 'the Kent miners were the poorest

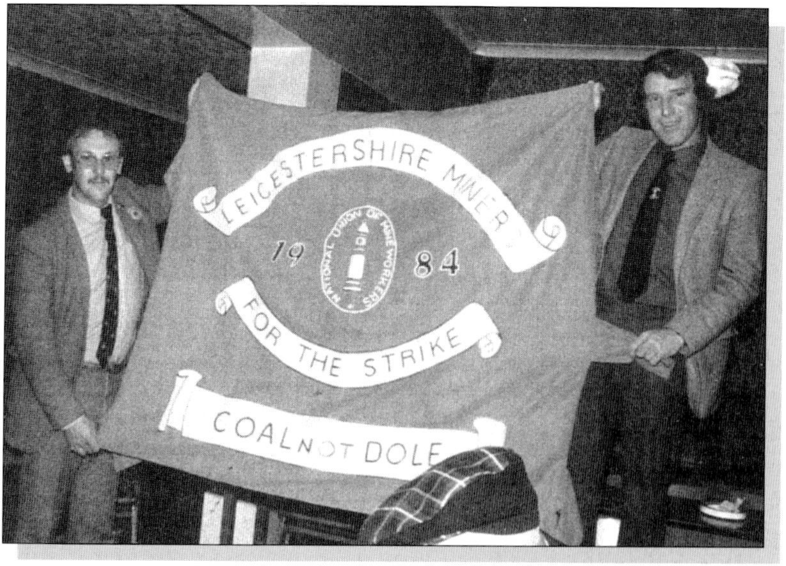

Mick Richmond and Malcolm Pinnegar with the Dirty Thirty banner

paid in the land, but it wasn't long before they were the best paid.'

As Malcolm saw the pickets outside his Bagworth pit, he knew that he would not be going to work the next day. Crossing a picket line was completely against his code, and his way of life. He actually missed a meeting the next day when the Bagworth miners decided to support the strike, but their decision was quickly changed when the Leicestershire NUM officials advised the men not to strike. Most of the men went back to work, apart from Malcolm and a few others.

By Monday, Malcolm had joined the picket line. When it became clear that he was one of very few local men to strike, the Kent men persuaded him to go back to work for a week, so that he could get his colleagues to come out. Most refused to do so.

In all of Leicestershire's pits only 30 men went on strike. The working miners dubbed them the Dirty Thirty, but, in a similar way to the soldiers dubbed the Old Contemptibles, the band of strikers took on the label and wore it with pride. Malcolm remembers them all, and their names feature in his reminiscences: Mick Richmond, Mel Elcock, Sam and Bobby Girvan, Phil Smith, Cliff and Nigel Jeffery, Dave Douglas. The majority of the 30 were from Bagworth, three were from Ellistown, and a few were from other pits. 'In one mine, only one man joined us,' Malcolm recalls, 'and that man had some guts.'

The Dirty Thirty had a very difficult year. Their working colleagues and some of their neighbours gave them a hard time. Malcolm received anonymous phone calls threatening harm to his family and even threatening his life. One man, a working miner, broke into Malcolm's house one night, intent on beating him up. Malcolm was not intimidated, however. He pushed him to the ground and sat on him until the police arrived to arrest the intruder.

He speaks warmly of the support of his wife and daughters, although like many other people he had relatives who were on the other side. Many mining families were split in 1984, with brothers, or fathers and sons, on opposite sides. Malcolm speaks appreciatively of how his wife gave evidence at the case when his intruder was charged. 'When the man's lawyer told my wife that she was just saying the same things as me about the event, she just looked him in the eye and said, "Happen it's the truth then." She's a very quiet and shy person normally and I was dead proud of her.'

Although the vast majority of local miners did not support the Dirty Thirty, Malcolm is very warm in his praise for other Leicestershire people who did. 'Hundreds of people helped us raise funds,' he says, 'and the railwaymen – especially at the Coalville depot – were terrific. Many of them refused to handle coaltrucks, and they like us had to live in an area where the consensus was against them.' Another local railway depot arranged for a large box so that railwaymen could bring in tins of food for the striking miners. It was soon full, but one night an anti-strike saboteur took the childish action of ripping the labels off the tins.

David, a local supporter of the Dirty Thirty, recalls how, when collecting tins of food outside an Ashby supermarket under a banner that read BUY AN EXTRA TIN FOR THE STRIKING MINERS' FAMILIES, it was hard to predict the reactions of the public. 'One moment someone would tear up our leaflets or even spit at us,' he recalls, 'and then someone would thrust a £10 note into our hands. When a fierce-looking policewoman came up, we thought she was going to move us on, but she gave us a donation and said she was ashamed of what some officers were doing.' Malcolm was appalled by the behaviour of some of the police, especially those from the Met, although the local bobbies were not too bad. He insists that he saw a man he knew to be a soldier appear in the police lines in police uniform. One Ashby lady, perfectly respectable and very middle-class, told me that she was arrested while supporting the pickets, taken to a police station and subjected to a humiliating strip search 'to teach her a lesson'.

Malcolm Pinnegar mentioned to me an occasion when a lady came into the Dirty Thirty's office in Leicester. She explained that her elderly father had just died and left her a few hundred pounds, which she was donating to the cause. The strikers were reluctant to take her money but she insisted, saying that her dad had been in the 1926 General Strike and would want them to have it.

The Dirty Thirty travelled throughout the country, and even the USA, addressing audiences about the strike and the reasons for it. One day Malcolm would be speaking in a Sikh temple, another at a mass meeting at a miners' rally. Wherever he travelled, the mention of the gallant band of men known as the Dirty Thirty brought cheers and applause. He was somewhat surprised in one part of Scotland to have to address two groups of striking miners, one Catholic and the other Protestant. They were both supportive of the Dirty Thirty and generous with their donations but would not meet together in the same hall. Apparently they worked at different pits, too, one for each denomination! 'That's religion for you,' Malcolm said wryly.

There was some humour to be had even during the darkest days. When Malcolm discovered that his phone was being tapped, he took some pleasure in making phone calls with fictitious stories about masses of flying pickets that were coming to a named local pit. Within half an hour he would be laughing as vanloads of police would be tearing off to the peaceful location.

He mentioned with pleasure one Leicester supporter named Tony Stephens, who wrote a play about the Dirty Thirty called *The Sun On Their Backs*. It was performed locally and also in South Wales and in Australia.

The numbers of the Dirty Thirty did vary from time to time. Two working miners from Ellistown pit came out a few months into the strike, saying that their conscience would not let them continue to work while others were on strike. After the strike, Malcolm even discovered an old pit worker who had stayed at home for the full period of the strike, unknown to the other striking miners. 'Did the number go down as well as up?' I asked him innocently. 'It did not,' Malcolm replied. 'Not one member of the Dirty Thirty went back until the end.'

The strike ended in defeat for the strikers in March 1985. 'I saw many grown men, big tough miners, crying on that day,' Malcolm told me. 'It was not easy for us to go back down Bagworth pit with men who regarded us as the enemy. Actually, we were lucky at Bagworth, because the manager and one of his deputies were very fair and stamped down on any intimidation.' He says that the atmosphere at Bagworth may have been unpleasant, but that it was a nightmare at the other Leicestershire pits. The members of the Dirty Thirty in those pits were real heroes, he believes.

After the defeat, most of Britain's mines were closed down, reducing their number from 170 to 12. When Bagworth closed, Malcolm went to work in a mine at Keresley, near Coventry, until that was closed too in 1992. Malcolm, whose fundraising skills had been honed to perfection during the strike, went to work for Leicester City Football Club on their lottery scheme. In later years he worked as a lorry driver.

Malcolm does not regard himself as any sort of hero. If he is, he feels, there were 29 more, plus all the men and women who supported them at great risk to themselves. Some lost their jobs, and were blacklisted, and some had to put up with threats and intimidation. He still takes pride in leading the Dirty Thirty. 'I know what we did was right,' he concludes, 'and the working miners now know what we did was right. Some have even come up to me over the years and said so. My conscience is clear and I think that history will prove that the stand we took was the right one.'

So, should Malcolm Pinnegar be in a book of Leicestershire heroes? Some readers may disagree, but I think that a man who put up with intimidation, threats and poverty for over a year in order to follow his conscience deserves his inclusion.

17

Eliane Plewman

– courageous SOE agent in wartime France

In 1937, Eliane was a 20-year-old woman, lodging in a very ordinary house in a very ordinary cul-de-sac in Oadby. She worked as a translator for George Odom Ltd, a firm of Leicester clothing exporters in Albion Street. She was invaluable as a translator because she was bilingual in French and English, fluent in Spanish and could manage to get by in Portuguese. Eliane had been born Eliane Browne-Bartroli in Marseilles in 1917, the daughter of a Spanish mother and a British father. She had been educated in France and England, and had then moved to Leicester. She married Tom Plewman, a British army officer, in 1942.

When the SOE – the Special Operations Executive – were recruiting agents in February 1943, Eliane made an ideal candidate. Not only was she an excellent linguist, with French as her mother tongue, she had one other quality. Her interview notes state that, because of the occupation of France, Eliane hated the Germans violently. It was written of her that the German occupation of France 'was a constant and deeply personal source of anguish to her'. It was decided that the Leicester office worker would make an ideal courier in wartime France, and Eliane was sent for training.

She was taught how to use weapons – guns and grenades – then sent to Manchester Ringway for parachute training. Next, in the highlands of Scotland, her SOE education was continued as she learned how to kill commando-style. Her training was completed at an SOE 'finishing school' where she was taught the art of blending in while acting undercover. When Elizabeth Nicholas, author of *Death Be Not Proud*, asked Tom Plewman if he had ever tried to change Eliane's mind about her new mission, he replied that he wouldn't have dared. He added that if he had attempted to prevent her from doing what she was convinced was right, their marriage might not have survived.

In August 1943 Eliane left England for France. She was 25 years old. She flew to the Jura region with 161 Bomber Squadron, then parachuted down with a briefcase containing a million francs for the Maquis, the French resistance movement. On landing she found no sign of the resistance workers who were supposed to meet her. Ominously, they had been arrested by the Germans. She hid the bag of money and, using her considerable initiative, made several contacts of her own, and joined up with a local network. The money she had hidden was stolen; although she later returned and found the briefcase, it was empty.

Eliane was no longer using her own name but her codename 'Gaby'. Her work was based on the area of Marseilles, her native city. She was to courier messages between Marseilles, St Raphael and the coastal town of Roquebrune where her radio operator was situated. Blending in as a French housewife, she passed through checkpoints and mobile patrols. She is known to have transported over four hundred messages, sometimes by truck, sometimes by train. She maintained liaison between various resistance groups, met newly arrived agents from Britain, and carried documents and even equipment. On other occasions, she would be in a truck with resistance arms and explosives on board and almost relished the irony of giving lifts to German hitchhiking soldiers. She also went to parachute drops and undertook sabotage of German aircraft. Her tirelessness in the cause made hers one of the most successful sections, or circuits, in France. It was also one of the most perilous circuits as Marseilles was full of Nazis and their sympathisers.

Once, on a Marseilles tram, Eliane met her own brother, also a SOE agent. Learning that she was on a mission and was carrying a handbag full of explosives, he insisted on accompanying her, and together the brother and sister blew up a length of railway line. Sabotage of locomotives was one of the main occupations of Eliane's section, which was codenamed 'Monk'. One night they destroyed two, blowing up the first in a tunnel, then the second when it was sent to clear the wreckage of the first. This action closed the Toulon to Marseilles line for four days. In one month, January 1944, the Monk agents attacked 31 railway engines.

Eventually, Eliane and her network were betrayed. One of the resistance men had a girlfriend who was simultaneously the girlfriend of a Gestapo sympathiser, a Frenchman named Bousquet, later shot as a traitor. When the leader of Monk section turned up at Eliane's flat in Marseilles, intending to wait for her, he was shot dead by two Germans posing as gasmen. The men cleaned up the blood from the killing, then waited inside. When Eliane turned up, the Germans were waiting for her. She drew her gun but was taken before she could fire. She was now a prisoner of the Gestapo.

Gestapo torture techniques included beatings, holding prisoners' heads under water until their lungs were bursting, and using electric shocks to various part of the body. The Gestapo in Marseilles was known to be even more brutal and sadistic than their counterparts elsewhere. In the headquarters in the Rue Paradis, Eliane was tortured constantly for three weeks, but refused to talk. A fellow prisoner was later to say, 'Eliane suffered with dignity the tortures that were inflicted on her by those sinister butchers. She swore that she had never known us.' He also recalls how, in spite of her weak condition, she would sing at the top of her voice, thus encouraging the rest of the prisoners to hold on. A note in her personal SOE file states simply that

ELIANE PLEWMAN

Eliane Plewman 'was tortured but gave no names away', a mere seven words which convey a whole chapter of meaning.

After failing to get any information from their prisoner, the Gestapo sent her first to Baumettes prison in Marseilles, then on to Fresnes prison in Paris. On 12th May, Eliane and seven comrades, all women agents, were loaded onto a train and taken to Germany. Her companions included Odette Sansom, whose story was later filmed, and Noor Inayat-Khan, daughter of a Sufi poet and a descendant of the legendary Indian Muslim leader Tipu Sultan. They spent many months in a women's prison at Karlsruhe where they made friends with the German political prisoners, women who had been imprisoned for their anti-Nazi beliefs. By now Eliane had developed a strategy of guile. When the Nazi authorities approached her to co-operate, she said that she couldn't make a decision like that while feeling hungry. It was only after she had received a decent dinner – quite a contrast to the usual poor prison food – that she told them to take a running jump.

On 11th September 1944, Eliane and three of her companions were taken by train to Munich, and then another twenty miles on to Dachau concentration camp. They had to walk from the station to the camp, arriving at midnight on 12th September. The next morning, the four women – Eliane Plewman, Noor Inayat-Khan, Madelaine Dammerment and Yolande Beekman – were executed. They were made to kneel on the ground in the crematorium compound, then shot in the back of the head. Eliane was still only 26 years old when she died. Her immense personal courage and devotion to the cause of fighting the Nazis were recognised by the award of a posthumous King's Commendation and the French Croix de Guerre.

In 1975, Eliane's widower, Tom Plewman, by then living in Lutterworth, made a visit to Dachau to attend the unveiling of a plaque in honour of the four executed women. Tom died in

2000. James Odom, a director of the firm where Eliane had worked in Leicester, had never known what his former employee had done after leaving the firm. When he eventually learned of her story he was amazed. 'I didn't realise she had been involved with that,' he said. 'I remember her as a nice perky person. I could never have dreamed she would go on to be an agent. That really shows some guts.'

In 1993 Odette Sansom, who survived the war, paid a tribute to Eliane and her companions. 'They are all our sisters and mothers,' she told an audience of schoolchildren. 'You would not be able to learn and play in freedom today if such women had not stood their soft slender bodies before you and your future like protective steel shields throughout the fascist terrors.' Eliane Plewman, one-time office worker in Leicester, is undoubtedly a Leicestershire hero, a woman of incredible moral and physical courage.

18

Robert Bakewell

– innovative breeder of livestock in the 18th century

Robert Bakewell was a Leicestershire farmer who became famous through his achievements in the breeding of livestock. The son of a tenant farmer, Robert was born at Dishley Grange near Loughborough in 1725. He began his new ideas in stockbreeding as soon as he took over the farm on the death of his father in 1760. In the past, sheep had been bred for their wool and cattle for their leather, but he could see that changes were coming. The population was growing rapidly, and the enclosures of common land meant that there was much more pasture land available. A quarter of the farm was given over to arable farming and the rest to grass. He had sixty horses, one hundred and sixty cattle and four hundred sheep. He developed a new way of using canal water to irrigate his farm, so that he could flood his land when he needed to.

While his father was alive, Robert had travelled widely throughout England, Ireland and the Low Countries, studying methods of farming. In the past, livestock of both sexes grazed together in the fields and the breeding was haphazard and random. Robert decided to separate them, and to breed deliberately from selected stock, common practice now but a revolutionary idea in the 18th century. He began to develop new breeds of stock, with meat in mind as well as for their original purposes. The Dishley sheep, later known as the New Leicestershire, became renowned throughout Europe and America. He started the practice of offering his magnificent rams for stud. In 1786 he hired out twenty rams and made 1,000 guineas in stud fees, and in 1789 he made 1,200 guineas from just three rams. One single ram, named Two-pounder, is reputed to have earned him 1,200 guineas in just one year.

He also bred a new variety of longhorn cattle, said to be 'small, clean-boned, short-carcased and inclined to be fat'. It became known, not surprisingly, as the Dishley Longhorn. Another animal he bred was a black horse, developed both for use on farms and as a cavalry horse for the army.

His new methods attracted many visitors to Dishley Grange, and these were given lavish hospitality and entertained generously by Robert and his sister. In fact, their hospitality was so liberal that he was eventually declared bankrupt. Nevertheless his advances in selective breeding, now regarded as commonplace, mean that the name of Robert Bakewell is regarded as a hero in farming circles.

19

Jenny Pitman

– the trainer whose career is part of horse-racing legend

Jenny Harvey, as she was then, was born in 1946 at a farm near Hoby. She was the middle child of seven. Her home, Lodge Farm, had no electricity, no gas and no mains water. Her dad George was a tenant farmer and on his hundred acres he kept dairy cattle, bullocks, sheep and pigs, plus chickens and geese, so the whole family grew up surrounded by a wonderful assortment of animals. Jenny would follow her dad everywhere, helping to feed the pigs, weigh the cattlefood and shut up the chickens to keep the foxes out. They also had a working mare named Nelly who would pull the harrow or cartloads of mangels. Jenny used to sit on Nelly as she worked, revelling in the warmth and smell of the horse, listening to the creak of the harness, and moving with the sway of the motion. Loving horses started very early in Jenny's life.

Every spring, Nelly would produce a fine foal, its quality guaranteed by the careful inspection Jenny's dad had made of the stallion when it was brought to Lodge Farm earlier. Jenny watched as her father checked the stallion from every angle, looking for faults, seeing how it moved. She also learned at her dad's knee the technical language of horsemen. The Harveys also kept a couple of ponies, for the children to ride. Jenny's two older sisters were quite restrained in their riding. In Jenny's words, 'they stuck to pony club-approved activities,' but Jenny was a tomboy. She would play at cowboys-and-indians, the covered wagon being a trap attached to one of the ponies, with a couple of her younger siblings hanging on for dear life. At other times

Jenny Pitman OBE

Jenny would ride off at dawn with a friend, Geoffrey, and spend all morning chasing through woods and jumping hedges. She always says that riding bareback with reins and bridles made of plaited bailer twine taught her far more than official riding school lessons would have done.

The ponies were used for work as well as wild games. Jenny, her brother Joe and pal Geoffrey would ride them to drive heifers or bullocks along the Fosse Way to the outskirts of Leicester where her father rented some fields, then ride them back to Hoby. They didn't worry about riding down the main road, as there wasn't much traffic in those days and anyway the drivers would always slow down for the youngsters on their ponies and the herd of cattle. Apart from their own two ponies, Jenny had others to ride. George Harvey had a good reputation as a horseman, and often badly behaved ponies – 'rearers, bolters and nappers', Jenny calls them – were brought to Lodge Farm for reschooling. As Jenny was judged to have the best hands, she was the one who rode the rogue ponies first. She quickly learned how to deal with a pony that wanted to unseat her, and how to differentiate between a pony who was frightened and one who was 'trying it on'.

Jenny went to Hoby village school, then on to the Sarson Girls' Secondary Modern School in Melton Mowbray. This involved a bus journey, and Jenny admits that she often missed the bus 'accidentally on purpose' so that she could go home and work on the farm. 'The attendance officer used to call at Lodge Farm so often I thought he must be a relation,' she recalls.

She also went hunting with the Quorn, not to see foxes killed, but to enjoy the hell-for-leather ride across the countryside, jumping whatever hedges she happened to meet. The local landed gentry must have cringed with horror, she says, when the Harvey kids turned up on their shaggy ponies, and wearing an assortment of clothing, though the Hunt Master was always friendly and made them feel welcome. Jenny managed to fracture her skull at Syston gymkhana, when a pole fell on her, but that didn't stop her riding.

Despite her mum's attempts to get her interested in dolls, and later in lipstick, Jenny remained a tomboy and enjoyed scrumping apples, shooting her airgun and smoking the odd illicit cigarette. On one occasion in a dispute over a seat with an older boy on the school bus, Jenny punched him on the nose, making it bleed.

And then she saw the film *National Velvet*, where a young girl played by Elizabeth Taylor dresses up as a boy and wins the

Grand National. She was entranced, and it remains her favourite film. She began to go to horse shows, and enjoyed watching local show-jumper Ted Williams school his horses before the competitions, trotting them in circles and figures-of-eight. She then got a weekend job at a small riding stable at Brooksby Grange, a few miles down the road. She would arrive at 7 am, muck out the horses, and then ride out with the stable lads, taking the racehorses across the lanes and fields. She found that although she was higher off the ground, her experience with the rearers and bolters at home stood her in good stead. When she left school this weekend job became full-time, but when the trainer at Brooksby Grange left to set up his own training stables near Cheltenham, he and his wife asked Jenny if she'd like to go with them. Jenny, aged seventeen and Leicestershire born and bred, hesitated about leaving home, but the opportunity was too good. She packed her bags, caught a coach from Leicester bus station, and set off for Gloucestershire.

It was while she was working there that she met a trainee jockey from nearby racing stables, a boy named Richard Pitman. It was the classic story: she couldn't stand him at first, he asked her out to the pictures, and after a while they became an item. However, when Richard found out that champion jockey Fred Winter was retiring from racing to set up as a trainer in Lambourn, he was keen to join him. Richard got a position and then asked Jenny Harvey to come to Berkshire with him, to take a job at stables near his. Ignoring advice from her colleagues that she was too young at eighteen to settle down, Jenny agreed to accompany Richard. In 1965, Richard and Jenny were married at the Blessed Sacrament church in Leicester, Jenny first having to convert to her fiancé's Roman Catholicism.

It wasn't long before Jenny was a mother to two sons, Mark and Paul, and beginning to feel trapped in full-time domesticity and motherhood. She was really missing the horses. Then Richard and Jenny took a huge leap into the unknown. They sold their warm bungalow and bought a six-acre plot of land with stables and an unheated caravan. The idea was that Richard would continue racing, and Jenny would take in injured race horses that needed getting back to fitness, plus young horses that needed breaking in. Beginning with a gelding with an injured leg, the reputation of Jenny Pitman's horse hospital – known as Parva Stud – grew. All the knowledge gained in her early years began to pay off. The only snag was living in a cold caravan with two children. Fortunately, with the help of prize money earned by Richard when he rode the second-placed horse in the 1969 Grand National, they were able to build a bungalow on the Parva Stud land. Jenny took on two local lads to help in their spare time, and taught them both to ride, along with her own sons. Word spread that she was teaching riding and Fred Winter sent his daughter along for lessons.

After she had helped one horse back to health and improved its attitude to work, its owner, Lord Cadogan, was reluctant to have him back. He suggested that Jenny should keep him and train him for point-to-point racing. Jenny took the horse out hunting and trained him up, then entered him in a race where he beat the favourite. Jenny Pitman was ecstatic and the training bug had really bitten. The next year she was training eight point-to-point racehorses. In 1975, two significant things happened to the Pitman family. Richard retired from being a professional jockey and took a job commentating for the BBC. Jenny was persuaded to apply for a professional National Hunt trainers' licence. Although women had been allowed to hold training licences since 1966, very few had been granted, and Jenny was apprehensive. She needn't have worried; she got her licence. Once her horses began to win, owners started sending their horses to her.

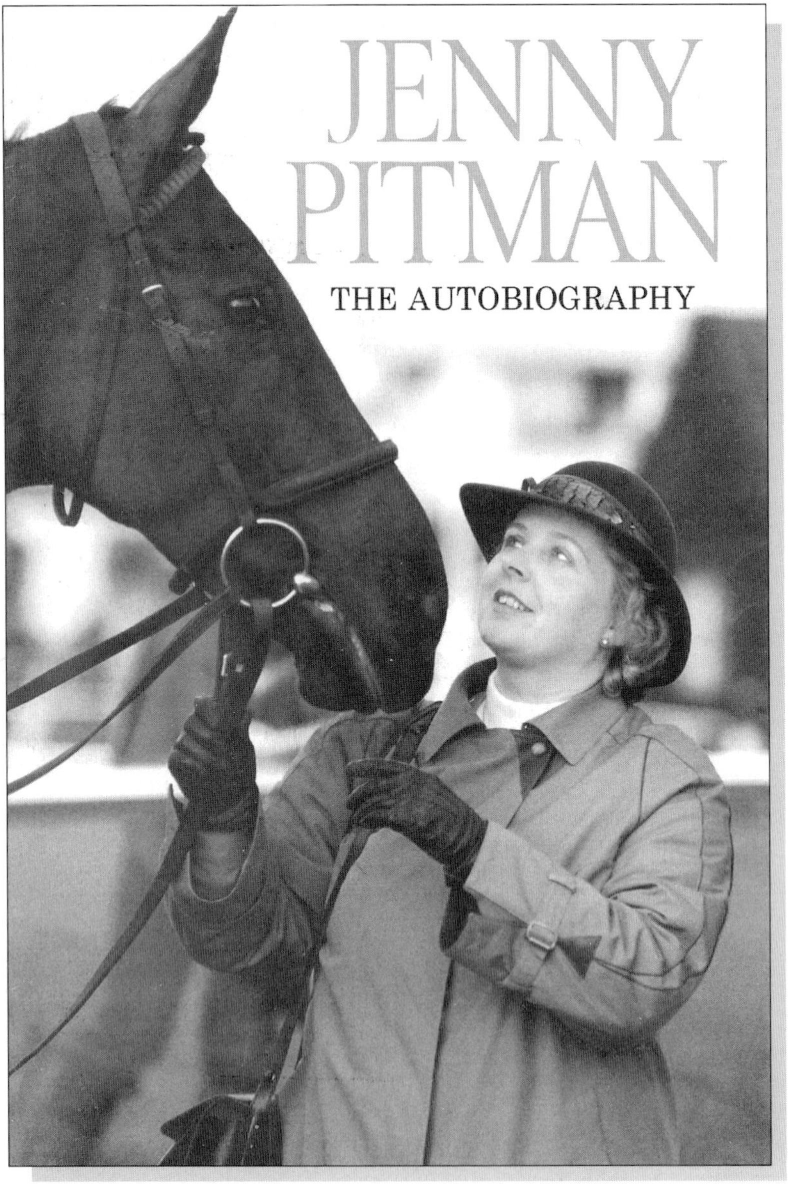
JENNY
PITMAN
THE AUTOBIOGRAPHY

Sadly, at the end of her first season as a trainer, Jenny's marriage broke up and Richard left. This meant that Parva Stud had to be sold and the money divided. Jenny had always felt that certain people round Lambourn looked down on her as a trainer because of her Leicestershire accent and the fact that she was a woman; she now felt that they would add her status as a divorcée to her list of faults. But she was always a doughty fighter and she began a new phase of her life.

Jenny had her sons with her of course, but professionally she was now on her own. Her career as a trainer is now part of horseracing legend. She trained the winners of all five major Nationals and two Cheltenham Gold Cups, once with *Burrough Hill Lad* – named after Burrough Hill in Leicestershire – and once with *Garrison Savannah*. In 1983 Jenny Pitman became the first woman trainer to have a winner in the Grand National, with *Corbierre*, and she repeated the feat in 1995 with *Royal Athlete*. Her son Mark became a successful jockey, riding many of his mother's horses, including the 1991 win in the Cheltenham Gold Cup. Mark then became a trainer himself, first as an assistant to Jenny, then in his own right. In 1997, Jenny married David Stait, to whom, she says, she had been engaged for eighteen years. She was awarded the OBE in 1998.

When asked what made her so successful as a trainer, Jenny Pitman, who retired from training in 1999, says that what she did was no different from other trainers, but she adds how important it is to keep a horse feeling happy. She always let a horse end the day on a playful note, having a bit of a buck in the yard or in the field. 'I wanted my horses to look out of their boxes and take an interest in life,' she says. She believes that if a horse is happy with life, he'll want to please you. That's just one of the tricks she learned from her dad in her family home back at Lodge Farm in rural Leicestershire.

20

Mary Linwood

– embroidery artist of international renown

Mary Linwood, who was born in 1755, moved to Leicester with her parents when she was five. Her father, a wine merchant, died within three years and her mother, Hannah, opened a day school in a house called the Priory on Belgrave Gate. On her mother's death in 1804, Mary took over the school and it continued to run for the next fifty years.

Mary began creating pictures in needlework when she was thirteen, and she was still doing so when she was 79. Many of her pictures were embroidered copies of paintings by famous contemporary artists – Gainsborough, Reynolds, Stubbs – and she developed a technique of conveying brushstrokes by using a mixture of long and short stitches. In 1766, her work was selected for the Royal Society of Arts exhibition in London. In later years, Mary had her own exhibition at the Pantheon in Oxford Street, and later in Hanover Square. A touring exhibition of her embroidery went to Edinburgh, Glasgow, Belfast, Dublin and Cork. Her work was much appreciated both in Britain and abroad. She met most of the crowned heads of Europe, and was one of very few artists to visit France during the Napoleonic Wars. In 1803, during an interval in the hostilities, she went to France, where she met the Emperor Napoleon and presented him with her portrait of him.

A collection of her work was exhibited in St Petersburg, where it attracted the attention of the Russian royal family, well known as great patrons of the arts. The Tsaritsa, Catherine the Great, offered Mary £40,000 for the whole collection while the Tsar was willing to pay 3,000 guineas for a single piece, *Salvator Mundi* or *Saviour of the World*. Mary refused both offers, explaining that she wanted her work to remain permanently in England, although at the request of the Russian Ambassador, she gave the Empress Catherine a picture for her palace. In 1790, Mary Linwood was awarded a medal for three of her pieces by the Society of Arts, and four years later was invited to an audience with Queen Charlotte and three of her daughters.

During her lifetime, Mary Linwood became the most successful and highly regarded embroidery artist. At her 1816 London exhibition, there were 64 of her pictures on display. However, despite her national and international fame, Mary continued to live in Leicester, running her school in Belgrave Gate, and visiting London just once a year to inspect her permanent exhibition there. Mary never married, and was the last person in Leicester to use a sedan chair to travel around the city.

She died of influenza at the age of 89 on 11th March 1845 and was buried in the south aisle of St Margaret's church. Her name was commemorated for many years by a school in Leicester that was named after her. This was not her own school in Belgrave Gate, of course, but a secondary school for girls, situated in the south of the city. A number of her embroidered pictures can still be seen in Leicester museums.

21

Linda Straw

– present-day textile artist and radical thinker

The contemporary equivalent of Mary Linwood is Linda Straw, who has lived in Leicestershire since 1961. Born in 1939, Linda has become one of the country's leading textile artists. Linda Neville, as she then was, went to Bristol grammar school, where she developed a passion for history, English literature and art. However, she frequently disagreed with the opinions of her teachers. She had a Marxist overview – she came from a socialist household – while she was taught by old-fashioned British Empire people. When Linda spoke of the oppression inherent in colonialism, they were outraged. As a result, her marks in history exams were always low. In English literature she clashed in the same way on the subject of Rider Haggard, when she questioned his outlook as shown in King Solomon's Mines. In art, her enthusiasm for the work of Stanley Spencer also went unappreciated. Amazingly, Linda came bottom of her class in both needlework and French; she has since become a highly acclaimed embroidery and quilting artist, and has taught in France, Belgium, Switzerland, Ireland, Holland, Germany and the USA!

Linda left school the day before her sixteenth birthday and had a number of jobs, the first being, she tells me, a 'nit-nurse's assistant'. She later gained an OND in opthalmics and did eye nursing. Other jobs have included sausage skin sorting and van driving. When she was doing the latter, making deliveries round Leicester, she sometimes made diversions to visit art galleries and museums, which led to her getting the sack. 'I must have been

Linda Straw

sacked from about fifty jobs in my time,' she tells me. 'Driving the van was so mind-numbing that I had a whole different life going on in my head.' Being fired – again – meant that Linda was now living on dole money but she at least she was able to devote all her time to her creative work. At this time her enthusiasm for art, literature and textiles came together and she began to spend her days using textiles to create pictures based on literary themes. It is difficult to know what to call Linda Straw's work; they are often called quilts, wall hangings or less glamorously 'stuffed

Detail from Linda Straw's A Midsummer Night's Dream

appliqué', but they are in reality huge works of art, paintings in textiles.

With no art training Linda developed her own method of obtaining the effects she wanted. The technique she developed, through a system of trial and error, is now taught in City and Guild courses and is – not surprisingly – known as the Linda Straw Method.

In 1981 Linda was using a sewing machine made by the Japanese company Riccar, and the UK managing director of the firm got to hear about her unusual technique, via the shop where she had bought the machine. He came to Linda's home in Leicester to see what she was doing, and was both amazed and impressed. The picture he saw was based on Shakespeare's *A Midsummer Night's Dream*. He bought it immediately and put it on display in Harrogate, before taking it to its present home in Tokyo. As a result, Linda was also offered a job teaching her methods in Ireland, and was able to become a full-time artist and teacher.

Other of Linda's works include *Romeo and Juliet*, *King Lear*, *The Tempest*, Dylan Thomas's *Under Milk Wood*, Chaucer's *Canterbury Tales*, and *The Mabinogian*. One award winning picture was called *1588 And All That: The Armada Quilt*, and a work commissioned by Madeira Threads to commemorate the Millennium was entitled *1000 Years of British History*. The Millennium Tapestry included not only Linda's work but also work by other quilters and embroiderers. Linda provided some 85% of the finished article, and she had the task of pulling it all together. This commission took four years to complete and was 35 ft wide.

Most of Linda's pictures are on a large scale. The *Romeo and Juliet* quilt is nine feet square and features seven scenes from the play, including Juliet's tragic death by the bier of Romeo, and the newly married lovers sporting naked on a couch. As with all Linda Straw's pictures, each time you go back and look, more details become evident. What I initially took to be Juliet's nurse sleeping nearby is, in fact, her doll. In between the main scenes are other figures. Queen Mab, the fairy spinner of dreams, looks on mischievously, and William Shakespeare himself sits contemplating his creation.

In another picture, a small side panel shows an elderly Queen Elizabeth I being comforted by Linda Straw! Linda's work is full of humour and wit, as well as compassion and humanity. Running through her work is, Linda says, 'an acknowledgement of our great debt to previous artists and the humour of life.' Her influences include illustrators Arthur Rackham, Edmund Dulac and Walter Crane, and painters Stanley Spencer and Pieter Brueghel, the 16th-century Flemish artist. What is known as 'stump work' from the Stuart era, with its padded shapes and applied motifs, is another source of inspiration.

Amazingly, Linda's technique – the now famous Linda Straw Method – involves much of the work being done from the back of the picture. In her own words: 'the work is drawn on paper and transferred onto fine vilene, the latter being incorporated within the work. Sewing from the back, through the design, the wadding, the silk fabric and appliqué silk, the work takes shape. Only when the appliqué is all in place do I turn over to embellish and embroider on the front.' Linda works with rich textiles, silk, velvet, satin, and finds that one of the advantages of living in Leicestershire is the availability of a variety of materials in the many sari shops in Leicester's Belgrave Road.

When I visited Linda in her large, rambling home, Georgian with gothic Victorian additions, one of the first things I noticed was a costume she had recently made, covered in illustrations based on the Book of Revelations. The four horsemen of the apocalypse were certainly there. 'I don't know what that St John was on,' she laughed, ' but he was definitely on something!' She shares The Tower House in the village of Lubenham with her son, her daughter-in-law, and her grandchildren, using the first floor studio for the renowned workshop courses she runs. She is also a self-taught cook and has started to do catering for 'posh parties' at her home.

When Linda and her family first bought the property, she says that it was like a scene from Sleeping Beauty, as they had to hack down decades of overgrown trees and shrubs to reach the house within. The garden is still only partially tamed. She refers to the area near the house – a haven for birds and animals – as the wild garden, but then adds that the further parts are her even wilder garden.

Linda has always been something of a rebel, doing her own thing. When she began her figurative work, the prevailing fashion among textile artists was for abstract designs, but she stuck to her preferred pictorial narrative style. When she researched 17th-century stump work, the librarians were scathingly dismissive; she was told that no one had taken it seriously for centuries. Again Linda ignored the mainstream advice. I also think that she must have caused something of a sensation among the more sedate needlework groups in the days when she would turn up at festivals, with all her materials, on the pillion of a large motorcycle.

She says that she rejects divisive and chauvinistic elements in society, and embraces the diversity and richness derived from both the isolation and the interaction of different cultures. Philosophically, she is still a radical in her views, supporting causes she believes in, whether they are popular or not. She is her own person. That is what makes Linda Straw one of my Leicestershire heroes.

22

Daniel Lambert

– 'the heaviest man who ever lived'

People have always been curious about fellow-humans who are in some way out of the ordinary. Long before the American freak shows were invented, anyone of unusual size or shape was regarded with fascination. They were given the title of 'rarities of nature', a less unpleasant epithet than 'freaks'. Leicester had one of the largest human beings who ever lived, Daniel Lambert, and also a man who suffered from an extreme case of neurofibromatosis, Joseph Merrick (see next chapter). Both men bore their physical differences, in the second case his deformities, with fortitude and stoicism that amounted to heroism.

Daniel Lambert, who became the keeper at Leicester jail, weighed over 50 stones. He was born in Blue Boar Lane, Leicester, in March 1770. He had two sisters who were, like his parents, of normal size, though he did have an uncle and aunt on his father's side of the family who were described as being very large, which suggests that his size may well have had a genetic cause. The uncle was described as the largest man in Leicester, but Daniel was later to take over that title. As a boy Daniel was tall and well built, but not unusually heavy. He liked sport and was a keen swimmer.

Originally apprenticed to a button engraver in Birmingham, Daniel returned to Leicester at the age of eighteen to assist his father, who was the keeper of the county bridewell, the 'house of correction', in Blue Boar Lane. Three years later, he took over his father's position as the jail keeper. He was still of normal size,

Daniel Lambert (courtesy of Joe Pie Picture Library)

about 5 ft 11 ins tall, and enjoyed a full social life. He bred dogs and fighting cocks, took part in hunting and other field sports, and was in appearance a sturdy but athletic man. However, during the next two years something abnormal happened, and by 1793 his weight had shot up to 32 stones and was still increasing. This had nothing to do with his intake of food and drink, since he was not greedy in his eating habits, eating only one course at any meal, and he never drank alcohol. He remained at this time a strong man, and was reported to be able to easily lift a weight of a quarter of a ton.

In 1805, when Daniel was 35 years of age, he had reached 53 stones in weight. When the prison where he worked closed, his employers declared 'the universal satisfaction Daniel Lambert had given in the discharge of the duties of his office.' However, he was not offered the post at the new prison, almost certainly because of his size. The Leicester magistrates granted him a life pension of £50 per annum, but this was not enough to keep him in comfort. His only option was to make money by offering himself for public exhibition.

After a carriage had been specially made to transport him, he moved to London, there taking apartments at 53 Piccadilly and later at 4 Leicester Square. He received visitors between the hours of 11 am and 5 pm, charging them a shilling to come and see 'the heaviest man who ever lived'. This rather high fee was, it was said, to keep out the riffraff. With a body circumference of over nine feet, and each leg having a circumference of over three feet, Daniel Lambert proved a great attraction with Londoners. He was reported to receive his paying guests with great courtesy, conversing with them with wit and conviviality. One visitor later wrote: 'When sitting, he appears to be a stupendous mass of flesh, for his thighs are so covered by his belly that nothing but his knees are to be seen, while the flesh of his legs, which resemble pillows, projects in such a manner as to nearly bury his feet.'

While he was in London, he met another Leicestershire man, the artist Ben Marshall. After Marshall had painted Daniel Lambert's portrait, the two men became good friends, the artist even naming one of his sons Lambert. However, being a curiosity on show may not have been entirely to Daniel's taste, since after only five months in London, he decided to return to a quieter life in Leicester, where he lived for another four years. He did not allow his great size and weight to restrict him to one place and, using his special carriage, he travelled to Birmingham, Coventry, Cambridge and Huntingdon. Daniel had a passion for horseracing, and he actually died on a visit to Stamford races at the age of 39, while staying in ground floor rooms in the Waggon and Horses.

To remove his body from the inn, the wall and window of the building had to be removed. It was decided to bury Daniel in Stamford, as returning him to Leicester would involve too many logistical difficulties. His enormous coffin was 4 ft wide and built from 112 ft of elm. Mounted on wheels, it was taken down a ramp to the grave in the churchyard, where it took twenty men thirty minutes to slowly lower him to his final resting-place. A gravestone erected by his many Leicester friends marks his grave in St Martin's churchyard.

In the Newarke Houses Museum in Leicester visitors can see his enormous waistcoat and breeches, together with his armchair and walking stick. Also in the museum is the portrait by Ben Marshall and a collection of caricatures. Despite the fact that the big Leicester man was a teetotaller, the city has a Daniel Lambert pub in Gamel Road, while Stamford has one in St Leonard's Street.

23

Joseph Merrick

– the so-called 'Elephant Man' who faced his disability with heroic courage

It might have been hoped that by the time of Queen Victoria, public attitudes towards 'rarities of nature' might have improved since the days of Daniel Lambert. However, the life of Joseph Merrick, born in Lee Street, Leicester in 1862 proves otherwise. If the name Merrick seems unknown, then his cruel nickname 'The Elephant Man' might give a clue to his identity.

Although Joseph appeared normal at birth, deformities soon began to appear on his face and body. A bony lump grew on his forehead and his lower lip began to swell. His skin became loose and coarse, his feet and right arm grew unusually large. Tumours were growing in the layers of his skin. As if this were not enough, his left hip was injured, causing him to limp. His mother Mary died when he was eleven and his father re-married, opening a shop in Russell Square with his new wife. Joseph's stepmother found him repulsive, and his father's attitude was not much better.

Joseph left school – Syston Street Board School – at the age of twelve, and found work in a Leicester cigar factory. After two years he lost this job because of his physical handicaps and his facial disfigurements, and at the age of fourteen he began to hawk from door to door, selling stockings and gloves from his father's haberdashery shop. Because of problems at home – his father was violent and his stepmother loathed him – Joseph moved out and went to live with an uncle who lived above his barber's shop in Churchgate. He continued to sell door to door until his strange appearance, and the crowds that gathered to stare and mock whenever he went out, led the authorities to withdraw his hawker's licence.

At the age of seventeen, Joseph went to live for five years in a workhouse in Sparkenhoe Street. By now, the growth from Joseph's upper lip resembled the trunk of an elephant. When he was twenty, a surgeon at Leicester Infirmary operated, and successfully removed part of this growth. However, he was still grossly disfigured and two years later Joseph Merrick made a heartbreaking decision. Like Daniel Lambert, 78 years earlier, he decided to become an exhibit. If his appearance could not be further improved, he had better make a living from it. He contacted a local musical hall promoter, Sam Torr, who was only too pleased to help. Joseph Carey Merrick became 'The Elephant Man'. Under the eye-catching slogan 'Half a man, half an elephant', he was put on show in Leicester and in Nottingham. Later, a showman called Tom Norman took him to London, and he became an exhibit in the capital. Among those who went to stare was a medical man with more a serious interest in the man on show. A surgeon from a local hospital, Frederick Treves, spoke to Joseph about his affliction, and left him with his card.

The attitudes of the time were changing, however, and the London police decided to close down the Elephant Man exhibition. Joseph's promoters did not want to lose their source of income, so they despatched him to Europe. To their annoyance they found that the police on the Continent were also turning against freak shows. Joseph's nightmare existence came to a peak when, in 1886, his manager decided to get out. He left with all the money, leaving the Leicester man stranded in Brussels with no job, no cash and nowhere to live. The Belgian police sent him back to London, where the English police were unsure what to do with him. Fortunately they found in his pocket the card the surgeon had left. Frederick Treves was contacted and he came to

Joseph's rescue, taking the so-called Elephant Man back to the hospital where he worked.

A subscription appeal was launched in *The Times*, and the money raised allowed Joseph Merrick spent the rest of his life in relative comfort. He received many important visitors, including the Prince of Wales. He may have been to some degree still on show, but at least the visitors were more distinguished. He was only 27 years old when he died in April 1890. A play was written about Joseph Merrick's sad life in 1977, and was put on in Leicester. Three years later, this was made into a film, *The Elephant Man*, starring the distinguished actor John Hurt in the title role. It was his sensitive performance that brought the story of Joseph Merrick's heroic courage and fortitude in the face of horrendous misfortune to the attention of the public.

24

Bob Miller

– Leicester fire fighter who lost his life while trying to save others

All fire fighters are, in my opinion, heroes. While the rest of us flee from most scenes of danger, particularly burning buildings, members of the fire and rescue service speed towards them. One such was Bob Miller, a 44-year-old father of two, based at Eastern Fire Station in Leicester. He was one of 70 fire fighters who were helping to tackle a fire in a disused Leicester hosiery factory in Morledge Street, in the early hours of Thursday, 31st October 2002.

He was one of the first men to go into the burning factory, to check whether there could have been people inside – squatters, people living rough or just trespassers. Bob fell through an open trapdoor and landed on a concrete floor twenty-five feet below. He suffered severe injuries to his skull and spine, killing him instantly. His death shocked not only the people of Leicestershire, but nationally. Ironically, he was killed at a time of talks between union officials and fire service representatives in an attempt to avoid a strike over pay and conditions, due to start in November. The fate of Bob Miller is a reminder to all of us just what we owe these everyday heroes. Bob, who had been in the fire service for twenty-five years, left a wife, Jane, and two teenage sons, Scott and Karl.

Bob Miller (Rob to his family but Bob to his colleagues) was a Leicestershire man through and through. He was born in South Wigston in 1958, the second of four children of Bill and Janet. He attended Guthlaxton School, then went into engineering but,

Bob Miller

according to his father, 'he decided that he didn't want to spend the rest of his life filing off bits of metal.' At eighteen, Bob followed his father and older brother Richard, by joining the Leicestershire fire service. He loved sport, and played rugby – becoming the captain of the brigade team – as well as cricket, soccer and volleyball. He also enjoyed rock-climbing and fishing.

The fire service is a family as well as a profession, and its members not only work as a team, they socialise together. Bob took part in all the fire brigade's fundraising activities, raising money for the benevolent fund, the Rainbow Children's Hospice and other charities. He was a key member of the back-up crew on a number of triathlon events, but insisted on cycling 70 miles of the course with the participants. He did a lot of the driving of fire fighters taking part in the Three Peaks Challenge – which involves climbing the highest mountains in England, Wales and Scotland within 24 hours.

Fire fighter Vince Cooper told me that Bob would always help a colleague who was moving house or needing some help around the home. Bob was invariably ready with a group hug if anyone had a problem in his or her life. 'In the brigade, all problems are shared problems,' he explained. Vince added that Bob was a master of the small practical joke. On one occasion, while doing some small household jobs for a colleague, he noticed that her cutlery drawer was far too neat, so decided to 'reorganise' it. He then proceeded to 'rearrange' her television set, but left it looking superficially normal. The colleague, Jan, was extremely puzzled when she came home and switched on, finding that something had caused the television picture to be upside down – until she recalled that Bob had been in the house!

Bob was a master at his professional job too, and received a commendation for rescuing two children and their mother from a burning house in Smedmore Road, a couple of years before the fatal Morledge Street fire. Bob was the first Leicestershire fire fighter to be killed on duty since 1977. He was mourned not only by his own family but also by his other family – his fire service colleagues. David Webb, the Chief Fire Officer of the Leicestershire service, who had been present at the fire, said, 'We are devastated. It sounds a bit of a cliché, but it is like losing a family member. These people have been friends for many, many years. People can imagine how bad it is from our perspective. It is the most tragic thing that can happen in the fire service – when we lose one of our own. Thankfully it is very rare.'

On Tuesday 12th November, thousands of people attended Bob Miller's funeral. Crowds of local people and fire fighters lined the streets for the procession as Bob's coffin, draped with a Union Jack, was taken from his fire station to Leicester Cathedral. His final journey was not in a hearse but, fittingly, on a turntable ladder vehicle. Colleagues from White Watch carried his coffin, surmounted with his medals and fire helmet, into the cathedral.

The service began with prayers led by the Very Reverend Vivienne Faull, the Dean of Leicester, followed by a tribute from David Webb. David told the hushed congregation, 'Bob was a big man, not just physically, but also as a person. He lost his life doing a job he loved, and working with people he respected and who respected him. He was held in high esteem by all of his colleagues and he will be remembered by many of them as a person they most wanted to be paired with at an incident. He lost his life fully convinced that he was trying to save the lives of others.'

As I said at the beginning, all fire fighters are heroes, men and women of courage, who risk their lives to rescue others. Bob Miller gave his life in doing his job, acting with bravery and selflessness. He is undoubtedly a Leicestershire hero.

Acknowledgements

I would like to acknowledge help from the *Leicester Mercury*, Ashby-de-la-Zouch library, Swadlincote library, Ashby Image & Print and the Three Owls Bookshop in Mill Lane Mews, Ashby-de-la-Zouch. I would also like to thank the following individuals: Peter Barrett, Colin Broadway, Vince Cooper, Adrian Cross, Steve English, Leslie Hextall, Penny Hopkins, Gillian Linscott, Bill and Janet Miller, Malcolm Pinnegar, Linda Straw, Sue Townsend, Paul Webster, Helen Wilkins and the Joe Pie Picture Library.

Bibliography

Bennett, J.D. Leicestershire Portraits (Leicestershire Libraries Service 1988)

Binney, Marcus The Women Who Lived For Danger (Hodder & Stoughton 2002)

Foss, Peter The History of Market Bosworth (Sycamore Press Ltd 1983)

Harker, Gail Fairytale Quilts & Embroidery (Merehurst Ltd 1992)

Johnson, JE 'Johnnie' Wing Leader (David & Charles 1956)

Johnson, JE and Lucas P.B. Winged Victory (Stanley Paul 1995)

Johnson, Martin Martin Johnson: The Autobiography (Headline 2003)

Nicholas, Elizabeth Death Be Not Proud (Cresset Press 1958)

Pitman, Jenny Jenny Pitman: The Autobiography (Partridge Press 1998)

Pudney, John The Thomas Cook Story (Michael Joseph 1953)

Raftery, Michael The Writers of Leicestershire (Leicestershire Libraries Service 1984)

Sarkar, Dilip Johnnie Johnson: Spitfire Top Gun (Ramrod Publications 2002)

Seaton, Derek The Local Legacy of Thomas Cook (Seaton 1996)

Snelling, Stephen Passchendaele 1917 (Sutton Publishing Ltd 1998)

Walker, Michelle The Passionate Quilter (Ebury Press 1990)

Index